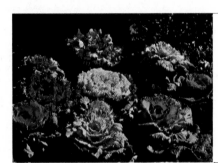

Written, edited and designed by the editorial staff of ORTHO Books.

Gardening Shortcuts

D1308860

Contents

From the first-hand experience of many

We build a book of good ideas from the experience of University Extension Specialists; from trials and errors in our own test stations; from gardeners as fresh as a seedling tomato and as sharp as an old-timer's hoe.

◁

We look at rooftops, high in the sky, for ideas in gardening where there is no space to garden.

Introduction

This book was gathered rather than written. It gathers a few hundred good ideas from good gardeners everywhere. Gardeners with and without titles who are finding ways to make gardening more enjoyable even when they talk about the frustrations of gardening.

The title of this book—Shortcuts—may suggest that it contains ideas that will cut short something. We hope that it will cut short the thought that gardening is an art requiring a long apprenticeship. We think that you can move into gardening or any specialized part of it, right now, and start at the top.

The conceit of this book is that it can single out the stumbling blocks that trip up good people intent upon growing something and remove the stumbling blocks before they stumble.

We like to think that there are gardeners who have read of the easy way to success in growing vegetables and flowers and such, who would welcome some talk about the hazards and stumbling blocks along the way.

In the next few pages we try to acknowledge some of the help we have received. Photographs of gardening plots in arboretums, in University Extension Stations and family gardens acknowledge the source of some of the ideas.

The camera takes a quick look at our own test stations and the gardens of friends where ideas (and seeds) from seed houses and new garden devices from manufacturers are tried out.

We have used many people. And probably the best part of this book is where we have given these people a chance to voice their views.

They have found some bit of shining truth that should be added to the literature of gardening. We hope that this book does right by them as we ride roughshod through the stumbling blocks in growing vegetables, flowers, bulbs, herbs or whatever; indoors, outdoors, skyward, downward and all around the house, townhouse or high-rise. When we talk of vertical gardens, raised beds, drip irrigation, kinder-gardeners, black plastic mulch and gardeners with a light heart; when we do right by the County Extension Agent, Mrs. Koehler of the National Oleander Society, and Gus Gagis of Wayne, New Jersey.

To the many who have helped us remove the stumbling blocks in gathering this book, our best thank you.

We talk of pole beans where the vines grow tall and the snap beans are brittle. A new variety? Purple pods?

And, far from the high-rise, in the finest garden spot in Utah, the solid know-how of the seasoned gardener.

Top and center left: Garden of All Seasons in Los Angeles State and County Arboretum. Here volunteers do their own thing in trying out vegetables, flowers, bulbs and mixtures of the same. This collection of small gardens has become a favored stopover for visitors to the Arboretum. The first stop for 10 to 15 school field trips daily is the Garden of All Seasons. Lower left: Impossible corner in garden of inventor-photographer, Clyde Childress. Pyramid shaped vertical garden takes care of hard-to-plant corner. Above center: Dixon Springs Agricultural Center, the University of Illinois at Simpson, Illinois. Here plastic mulches get a thorough workout.

Upper left: County Extension Agent, Duane Hatch, makes major contact with the gardening public through testing planting methods, plastic mulches and variety trials in Eugene, Oregon.

Upper and lower right: After one year, the Ramsayer family of Ventura, California and their five boys have expanded their gardening activities to include a pre-fab greenhouse with lath overhead, raised beds, and pots, boxes, baskets and dwarf fruit trees all around the yard. Plenty of trial and error here with vegetables and flowers outdoors and in the greenhouse.

Top: Evergreen blackberries in bloom at North Willamette Experimental Station of the Oregon State University. This station (photos center right and top left of page 7) contributes up-to-date know how in growing blackberries, grapes and strawberries. Above left: Jack Chandler of St. Helena, California puts a series of raised beds to work in vegetable variety trials. Above right: Part of a garden workshop at the Home of Guiding Hands, a residential facility for the retarded at Lakeside, California. Horticultural therapy plays its part at the Home of Guiding Hands.

Top right: An overhead view of an experiment in vegetable growing in small space—containers, raised beds and vertical planting—in the garden of Joseph Parker, Hollywood, California. Below: At famous Callaway Gardens, Pine Mountain, Georgia, Mr. Cason's Vegetable Garden has been the All-American Trial Garden for vegetables since 1964. This is one of 26 trial gardens in the United States. Each year, new, unnamed or numbered varieties are grown to be evaluated and compared with standard named varieties presently available in the trade. All-America awards are given to high-scoring varieties of vegetables.

If your soil is hard to manage

Take one of these steps:
1) Amend the soil you have, whether too heavy or too light, by adding organic matter.
2) Forget it and (a) go to raised beds with special mix above ground within the bed (b) go to container growing, working with pots and boxes.

Soil

Anyone who has read the planting directions on a seed packet or a catalog is familiar with such instructions as "Sow seed in early spring as soon as the soil can be worked" and "Plant in a well-drained sandy loam."

How *early* is "as soon as the ground can be worked" in your garden? A rain-soaked heavy clay soil may not be ready for spading or tilling until spring gives way to summer.

Why the repeated emphasis on "good drainage"? When water replaces the air in the soil, roots suffocate. Roots will not develop without a constant supply of oxygen and a constant removal of carbon dioxide.

A well-drained soil is one in which the water moves through quickly never completely shutting off the movement of air through the soil.

A sandy soil is well drained but dries out quickly. Frequent watering washes nutrients through the soil.

The best advice a gardener ever had was "Don't try to live with an unfavorable soil." Nothing can dampen the enthusiasm of the beginner more quickly than a hard-to-manage soil.

The only quick way to change either a heavy clay soil or a light sandy soil to a substitute for a rich loam is through the addition of organic matter. Not just a little organic matter, but lots of it.

The addition of organic matter—compost, peat moss, manure, sawdust, ground bark—makes clay soils more mellow and easier to work.

Organic matter opens up tight clay soils, improves drainage and allows air to move more readily through the soil, warming it up earlier in the spring.

◁

Here's vegetable growing at its highest point. The practicality of raised beds, the pleasant geometry of vegetables in rows and the added elegance of turf covered paths.

In light sandy soils, organic matter holds moisture and nutrients in the root zone.

Don't confuse this massive addition of organic matter to the soil with the long-term improvement program that comes with the breakdown of organic matter into true humus (that final black sticky stuff that holds soil particles together in crumbs).

The quantity of organic matter must be large enough to physically change the structure of the soil. And *enough* means that at least ⅓ of the final mix is organic matter.

The definition of waste material is changing. Less and less of the green material is burned or buried. What comes out of the soil goes back into the soil to restore and improve it. Many "waste" products are now popular nursery items—sawdust, bark in all sizes, manure and more. But if you look around you may discover a waste product of agriculture that is peculiar to your area. And local agricultural by-products are usually less expensive than packaged and processed ones. Where grapes are pressed there is pomace. Where nuts are shelled there are shells which can be ground or pulverized. Where there's a cider mill there's apple pomace.

Composting

The objective of composting is to convert waste material into a sort of synthetic manure—dark brown crumbly stuff with the good-earth fragrance.

You take leaves, grass clippings, small prunings, straw, spoiled hay, sawdust, green weeds, dry weeds, vegetable harvest refuse, vegetable matter from the kitchen, coffee grounds, eggshells, shredded paper, wood ashes and pile them in such a way that soil bacteria can thrive and multiply and break down these waste materials into a form you can use.

The bacteria are the converters of the raw material and they must have a workable environment. They need moisture, air and food.

Grass clippings, green weeds, lettuce leaves, pea vines and other succulent materials contain sugar and proteins which are excellent nutrients for the bacteria. They decompose rapidly—sometimes too rapidly. However, dry leaves, small twigs, sawdust and like woody dry materials decompose very slowly unless the bacteria are supplied with extra nitrogen.

The size of the woody material will affect the rate of decomposition. If

In planting situations, such as rooftops, raised beds are the only solution to the space problem.

The raised bed idea works well in problem situations—especially with trellis devices, protection from birds, on hillsides, along fences and in awkward corners.

There are multiple benefits in planting in soil held above ground level. It allows for special soil mixes and assures good drainage. Results are apparent when any vegetable is harvested.

leaves, large and small, go into the pile as they are raked up, decomposition will be much slower than when shredded by a rotary mower.

Prunings, clippings, wood chips will take months to break down even with extra nitrogen. However, when put through a shredder, and mixed with green material, they will decompose rapidly.

THE CLASSIC LAYER CAKE. Gardeners have found that some form of a series of layers of waste material with fertilizers, manures and garden soil between the layers is the best way to build a compost pile.

The size of the pile will depend on the size of your garden. But two piles 4 by 6 are easier to manage than one 4 by 12.

You start the pile by spreading a layer of refuse about 6 to 8 inches thick over the 4 by 6-foot area. Spread over this layer a mixture of manure, garden soil and commercial fertilizers. This is the filling on the layer cake. And it's on the composition of this filling that composters have different opinions.

Both manure and a commercial fertilizer should be used to give the bacteria the food they need. The amount will be more if the waste material is dry rather than green. The greater the amount of fertilizer the richer will be the compost. A good average amount for each layer is 2 cupfuls of ammonium sulfate or blood meal.

Wet down the fertilizer layer just enough to carry the chemicals through the layer; don't wash them out with heavy watering.

In areas where the soil is on the acid side, the addition of a cupful of ground limestone, crushed oyster shell, or dolomite lime to each layer will give you a less acid product and improve decomposition as well.

Add another layer of vegetable matter, spread the soil-manure-chemical layer over it and wet it down. Repeat the layering process until you run out of material or the pile is 4 to 5 feet high.

Form a basin at the top for watering and to catch the rain.

Keep the pile as wet as a squeezed-out sponge. In a dry climate it may need water as often as every 4 to 5 days in warm weather.

Top: Many varieties lettuce make a beautiful display in raised beds.

Bottom: Special raised bed, for potatoes only planted towards the rear of the garden shown on page 8. Potatoes flourish in specially prepared soil.

Under normal conditions the pile should be turned in 2 or 3 weeks and again in 5 weeks. It should be ready to use in 3 months.

If the pile is built when the weather is warm you'll see heat waves rising above the pile in 24 to 30 hours. Turn the pile to mix the materials and follow up with a thorough watering. It will heat again, and in a few days be hot enough to require turning again. Each time you turn it, move outer materials towards the center where heat and moisture encourage decomposition.

Synthetic soil

Garden stores offer soil substitutes or synthetic soils that have many advantages over soil. They are clean, free of weed seeds and plant disease organisms. They are very lightweight.

As a growing medium for a wide variety of plants the mixes are almost foolproof. They can scarcely be water-logged. Excess water drains through rapidly. Plant roots will spread throughout the well-aerated "soil," rather than develop at the edge of the containers.

Cornell and the University of California pioneered in formulating standard "soil" mixes for commercial plant growers. Mixes, following their formulas, are available under several labels. Some of the nationally distributed brands are 'Jiffy Mix,' 'Redi

Earth,' 'Pro-Mix.' In the West the U.C. type mix is 'Super Soil.'

The basic difference between the original U.C. mix and the Cornell version was in the use of vermiculite in the Cornell mix and fine sand in the U.C. mix.

You can make your own 'soil' mix. If you are going to fill a few planter boxes, a half dozen large pots or plan on using it in raised beds, mix the largest amount that can be easily handled in one mixing operation. That will be about a yard or 27 cubic feet. The Cornell mix is made up of equal amounts of peat moss and vermiculite plus fertilizers.

Dampen peat moss and roughly mix it with the vermiculite. Spread these fertilizers over the pile: 5 pounds of 5-10-10 commercial fertilizer; 2 pounds of superphosphate; 5 pounds of agricultural lime.

Remember that thorough mixing is essential. Each portion of the mix, down to a 2-inch potful, must have the same ingredients—and you can't get that by stirring.

To make a substitute for the U.C. mix using easy-to-buy ingredients: To 1 part peat moss, 1 part fine sand, 1 part perlite, add 2 pounds single superphosphate, 1 pound sulfate of potash, and ½ pound of iron sulfate. Mix thoroughly as with the Cornell mix. In this formula the readily available sulfate of potash is substi-

This handsome raised bed framed with railroad ties, borrows space from the lawn. Planted with 'Moss curled' parsley and cabbage; a combination of good looks and good uses in the kicthen.

Raised beds

The simplest of raised beds is the furrow—to improve drainage and add depth to shallow soil.

first to drain
first to warm up

HARD PAN

Small logs, railroad ties, or telephone poles can add 8 inches or so to the soil depth of any area enclosed by them.

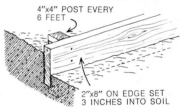

An open bottom box, tub, or pot works well in back of borders for those plants, like lilies, that require better than average drainage.

The formal raised bed—
For just a few inches of depth construction can be as simple as this...

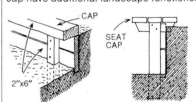

4"x4" POST EVERY 6 FEET

2"x8" ON EDGE SET 3 INCHES INTO SOIL

Deeper raised beds with a cap or seat cap have additional landscape functions.

CAP

SEAT CAP

2"x6"

Rock walls are less stiff and harsh than wooden raised beds—and you can plant in the cracks.

LEAN WALL 1 INCH FOR EACH FOOT OF HEIGHT. SLOPE ROCKS SO WATER FLOWS INTO SOIL BETWEEN THEM.

Something as simple as 3 or 4 rocks close together with the space between filled with soil is a great raised bed.

tuted for nitrate of potassium. Therefore the mix is without nitrogen.
In using it, start your feeding program
soon after planting. See page 13
for more about mixes.

This is the best method we know to
insure a thorough mix: start with a
pile of peat moss (dampened) and
vermiculite or perlite (depending on
which mix you are making). Mix a little
and then scatter the other ingredients
over the pile. Shoveling from this pile
start a cone-shaped pile by pouring
each shovelful directly on top so that
each shovelful dribbles down the
sides. Repeat the cone building
three times.

The raised bed

The raised bed has been around a
long time. The principle of above-
soil-level planting has been
applied throughout gardening
history. The raised soil was and is
"framed" with stone walls, brick,
logs, adobe, railroad ties, concrete
and boards of all dimensions.

Landscape architects and gardeners
who have tried raised beds point out
these virtues:

✔ *SPEEDS UP SPRING PLANTING.*
In a wet cool spring the soil in the
raised bed will warm up and be ready
for planting weeks before regular
garden soils can be planted.

✔ *NEVER TOO MUCH RAIN.* With
soil raised above ground level,
drainage away from the bed is possible. Unless the soil around the bed
is flooded, the raised bed will never
be waterlogged.

✔ *NO-KNEEL GARDENS.* You sit on
the edge of the raised beds when

weeding. Cultivating can be done with
a putty knife instead of a hoe.

✔ *ALWAYS NEATER.* As a clean and
neat structure, the gardener feels an
obligation to keep the planting clean
and neat. Weeds are more distracting
in a raised bed than an equal amount
of planting space in a hidden corner
of the garden.

✔ *GIVES ORDER TO THE GARDEN.*
The color of flowers and vegetables
comes and goes with the seasons; the
raised bed can be an attractive element in the garden in spring, summer, fall and winter.

✔ *PETS OF SPECIALISTS.* Herb
gardeners, collectors of miniatures in
bulbs, cactus and succulents or
whatever, appreciate the restraint
and the close-to-the-eye level of the
raised bed.

✔ *WHEELCHAIR GARDENS.* Raised
beds can be adjusted to wheel chair
height and make gardening available
to all who find it satisfying.

*In addition to putting an end to muddy
feet, boards prevent soil compaction; can
be used to cover seeds in first few days
of germination to retain moisture.*

*From the "Hatch Patch" demonstration garden in Eugene, Oregon: Left: To save seed and to insure uniform spacing, hole is made
with the end of a hoe, a few seeds are dropped in and a pinch of vermiculite placed over them to prevent soil from crusting. Center: Plants
emerge in a clump and are spaced uniformly. Right: By transplanting seedlings from clump, "thinning" is taken care of without waste.*

Concentrate

With a yard or so of lovely soil-mix on hand you find yourself using it in more ways than in raised beds and containers.

When setting out transplants or seeding a few plants of tomatoes, peppers, squash or the like, prepare individual planting holes and fill with the mix.

Before sowing beans or any seeds which are difficult to start in heavy soils, fill the seed row with the mix. Follow the lead of many growers using the "plug" method: Sow seeds of corn, melons and almost any vegetable in a handful of damp mix and plug mix and all into the row or hill at the proper spacing.

Above, vermiculite over seed row prevents crusting of soil. Below, a mixture of peat moss and vermiculite being used in the row for the same purpose.

When sowing seed in less than ideal soil, make deep furrows and fill with the mix. Seed germination will be faster and there will be no trouble from soil crusting.

Soil crusting

Anyone who has sown seeds in soil or soil mix in which there is even a small amount of clay knows what crusting means. After every rain or garden sprinkling the small clay particles bind the top of the soil and form a crust. When dry the crust shuts off air to roots, repels water, and locks in emerging seedlings. To prevent formation of crust over seed rows, cover the seeded rows with a thin mulch of vermiculite or other light mulch. Mulch breaks the force of drops of water that binds the minute clay particles to form the crust.

Green manure

Of the many ways to improve the soils —composts, organic matter of all kinds—there is an important one that is too often overlooked by the vegetable grower—the growing of legumes and grasses as a cover crop to be tilled into the soil. They, the good farmer says, are the green manures.

What legume—clover, vetch, etc., —you plant or what grass will depend on the climate and season of the year.

Using cover crops in the small garden means that no part of the garden remains idle. The cover crops take over when any space is open.

These words from one of our gardeners are in support of the green manures:

"After using many methods of soil improvement I still come back to a cover crop for my garden. I plant oats and vetch as early as feasible in the fall, and turn it under as late as possible in the spring. The first year I tilled the crop under, the crop was so thick that it completely fouled the rototiller. The answer, with or without a rototiller, is to mow the crop a day or two before turning it under— it cuts the work in half."

More about the planter mixes

Unless the sterilized packaged mixes such as Jiffy-Mix, Pro-Mix, Redi-Earth and Super Soil are used straight without adulteration, such as extending them with garden soil, the value of sterilization is lost.

If you wish to add compost or garden soil they should be sterilized. Small quantities of compost or soil can be sterilized by baking in the oven. Some of the mess and odor that went with this operation in the past can be avoided by using the large plastic bags sold for oven cooking (turkey bags). The more shallow the soil in the bag, the shorter the baking time. The soil is done (sterilized) when all of it reaches 180°; all of it may reach that temperature in 45 minutes in an oven set at 350°. Don't overcook—overcooking can release toxic substances in the soil.

The camera catches the critical moment in the birth of a bean, (top) pulling the swollen seed, now heavy with water through the soil. Then the seedling breaks through and spreads its pair of primary leaves.

Water... the hazardous necessity

Plants can't live without it but they can be killed with an excess of it.

Who ever called water the "hazardous necessity" knew what he was talking about.

The chances are about 90 to 10 that if you show a plant—be it shrub, tree, herb, flower or vegetable—to a plant doctor, the diagnosis will be either "too much water," "too little water," or "bad watering habits."

And the chances are equally good that the plant doctor would be right. And more often than not, it would be "too much water."

Of all the lines in all the chapters and volumes of advice to gardeners, the most confusing and the most frustrating are those relating to watering, (and these pages may not clear the air).

Ask why the tomato blossoms dropped and among other reasons you are told "Either too much or too little water." Ask why your carrots are cracking, or your cactus dying, or why the yellowing leaves on the azaleas, and you are warned against overwatering. Ask about bitterness in lettuce and you are warned against an uneven supply of water.

What's "too much" and "too little"? One answer: The phrase "too much water" is used in two ways. Too much water for the roots to grow in; and a supply of water (moisture) that gives the plant maximum leaf growth, rather than fruit.

When water is called the "hazardous necessity," it means that you can kill a plant right fast with water. Plant roots require moisture and air for growth. They require a growing medium in which air can move through bringing oxygen for their growth and removing the carbon dioxide they respire.

Stop the supply of air, by filling all of the air spaces in the soil with water, and root growth stops. The longer time that air is cut off, the greater the damage.

Damaged roots have little defense against the entrance of rot-causing

○
Every gardener has his favorite way of irrigating. Soil type and garden layout are deciding factors. It's right if the harvests are right.

soil organisms. And so the plant dies of root rot.

Another series of warnings of the hazards of water comes at the reader of garden advice in the planting directions for the various vegetables. "Plant in a *well-drained,* rich, loamy soil," or "Does best in a light, well drained soil."

Such warnings mean that the plant is easily damaged by too much water.

The gardener with good watering habits learns to apply water according to the nature of his soil. There is *no way to half wet the soil.* You prevent over-watering by making the intervals between watering fit the water holding capacity of the soil.

Soils on the clay side have a high water holding capacity, the air spaces are minute, and water moves through them slowly.

Such soils need infrequent watering. The gardener who manages them learns to use the spade test, to look at and feel the soil beneath the surface inches.

The very best way to solve the problem of water management is to prepare a garden soil that can't be over-watered. (See Soil, pages 8-13.)

If there is one justification for saying "I just haven't got a green thumb" it's in the watering department with problem soils (the soils most gardeners have). It takes time to know the watering needs of each plant and to water deeply or shallowly, frequently or infrequently, plant by plant. When soils in the garden vary the job becomes more complicated.

The specialists have a useful word about water and plant growth generally. It's a word everyone knows— *stress.* A plant that is not getting its full quota of water is under *water stress.* As the moisture supply in the soil decreases, the plant must work harder. Water stress is progressive, slight to severe. In a dry year many street trees and forest trees suffering from water stress become fair game for the stress from insect damage.

In the vegetable garden water stress is something you don't want—except on rare occasions such as the tomato that insists on vine production only and no fruit.

Water stress affects various vegetables in special ways. A cucumber under stress just stops growing and when water is supplied again, resumes growth.

When sweet corn is tasseling is no time for water stress.

When potatoes are on an uneven watering schedule you get knobby potatoes.

Plantings of vine crops such as squash and pumpkins require much more vine space than root space. When the soil is not the best, the soil improvement can be concentrated in the root zone area. Here the gardener has prepared special soil mix in the root zone.

Water is concentrated in the root zone of this happy zucchini using a bottomless coffee can sunk in the ground.

Deep furrow irrigation with melons. Root zone is watered without wetting the adjoining soil. Vines are trained away from the furrow so that melons are on dry ground.

Drip, trickle, emit, ooze

New systems to do better what good gardeners have done for years—give the root system, and only the root system, what it needs for growth.

The principle of making a little water go a long way is not new to the home gardener—especially those with limited water supplies. They found out what the drip irrigators are finding out: when only a portion of the root system of a plant receives the water it needs, the plant will thrive. The home gardener did it with coffee cans, draintiles and such.

Today gardeners are hearing new words about irrigation techniques and equipment—such as emitters, spot-spitters, Dew-Hose, Jumbo-oozers, Viaflow, Twin-wall, Drip-Eze are a few. After years of testing in thousands of acres of orchards, row crops, nursery operations, the drip/trickle system of irrigation is being

Drip emitter, (above) takes care of new plantings in black plastic. Spot-Spitter (below) can deliver as dripper or spitter by changing the water pressure.

offered to the home gardener. The systems offered are not fool proof. Manufacturers are changing parts in the systems as more tests are made. But the potential advantages of drip irrigation in shrub and tree plantings, home orchards, vineyards and vegetable gardens are so great that the home garden experiment seems worthwhile.

On the following page we chart the workings of a composite automatic drip system as it is put together for various commercial uses. Home garden units are modifications of this system.

The advantages of drip irrigation are noted in the following quotes from Dr. Falih Aljibury, Irrigation and Water Technologist from the University of California:

"While generally considered as a new irrigation method, the basic concept of drip irrigation has been practiced since the beginning of this century by nurseries growing fruit trees and ornamental plants. However, it has only been in the past few years that this concept has been expanded to include application in many crops grown in the field as well as under nursery and greenhouse conditions.

Viaflo soaker-oozer (above) and close-up of section (below) as water passes through micron-sized pores in the walls, and moves uniformly into the root zone.

"With drip irrigation, the water drops onto the soil surface without disturbing the soil structure, so that the water can seep between soil particles. Once in the soil, the water moves by capillary to the surrounding areas.

"Drip irrigation drops the water onto the ground through one or more emitters located adjacent to each tree or plant.

"The wetting pattern developed under each emitter determines the number of emitters to be used per tree or plant. In drip irrigation about 40 to 50 percent of the allocated area per tree is wetted, as compared to nearly 100 percent with sprinkler irrigation.

"In other parts of the world, farmers attempt to wet no more than 40 percent of the tree area. However, at the present time researchers feel that this is too close a margin for U.S. farmers who have greater potential problems, as well as a generally greater availability of water.

"In drip irrigation one tries to replenish the water on an almost daily basis. This amount of water being equal to the water used by the plant or tree since the last irrigation. In other words, drip irrigation does not store water for a long future tree use, but rather constantly replaces water that has already been used. Mature citrus trees grown in the San Joaquin Valley could use up to 30 gallons per tree per day. Mature plum trees in the Valley use up to 50 and 60 gallons per day.

"*Drip components.* The basic components of a drip irrigation system consist of the head, laterals, emitters, and hose lines.

"The head, which connects the main water source to the laterals and drip hoses, generally consists of a number of components, such as control valves, couplings, filters, time-clocks, fertilizer injectors and gauges.

"Since water drops out through minute outlets in the emitters, the water must be very clean. Generally speaking, the water is passed through 160-mesh screens before it is distributed to the drip system.

"While there are good commercial drip irrigation systems available today, further technological development in filtration is desired. Also, further work is desirable to fully alleviate the problem of emitter plugging. The damage done by rodents chewing on the hose or emitters may require changes in construction materials."

Composite of drip irrigation systems

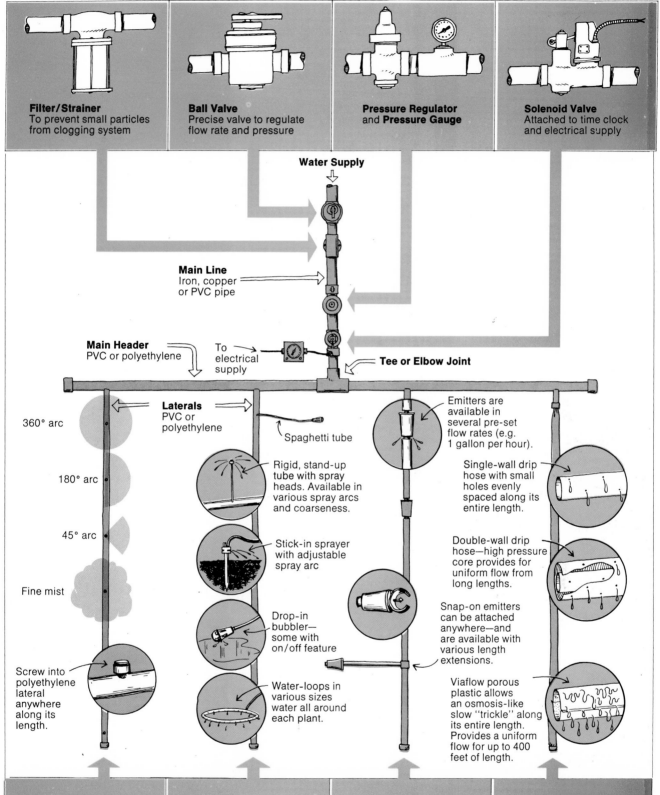

Filter/Strainer
To prevent small particles from clogging system

Ball Valve
Precise valve to regulate flow rate and pressure

Pressure Regulator and **Pressure Gauge**

Solenoid Valve
Attached to time clock and electrical supply

Water Supply

Main Line
Iron, copper or PVC pipe

Main Header
PVC or polyethylene

To electrical supply

Tee or Elbow Joint

Laterals
PVC or polyethylene

Spaghetti tube

360° arc

180° arc

45° arc

Fine mist

Screw into polyethylene lateral anywhere along its length.

Rigid, stand-up tube with spray heads. Available in various spray arcs and coarseness.

Stick-in sprayer with adjustable spray arc

Drop-in bubbler—some with on/off feature

Water-loops in various sizes water all around each plant.

Emitters are available in several pre-set flow rates (e.g. 1 gallon per hour).

Single-wall drip hose with small holes evenly spaced along its entire length.

Double-wall drip hose—high pressure core provides for uniform flow from long lengths.

Snap-on emitters can be attached anywhere—and are available with various length extensions.

Viaflow porous plastic allows an osmosis-like slow "trickle" along its entire length. Provides a uniform flow for up to 400 feet of length.

Screw-In Spray Heads
Screw into polyethylene pipe after guide hole is punched with an awl. Available in various pre-set spray arcs and with coarse spray, fine spray, or mist.

Spaghetti Tubes And Nozzles
Thin, plastic tubes cement into PVC pipe anywhere you punch a hole. Tube length is optional—usually 1 to 6 feet. Many nozzles are available for various growing situations.

Drip Emitters
Available pre-assembled into plastic pipe at regular intervals or as snap-in units for irregular installation. Provides small, steady, and *precise* amounts of water exactly where needed.

Soaker/Oozer
Perforated or porous tubing allows water to trickle from its entire length at a fairly uniform rate. Several kinds with different materials and systems are available for row plants and borders.

Water... at play

It drips, splashes, spills, surges, gurgles, reflects and sparkles to delight the eye and charm the ear.

How to make flowing water sing the song you want to hear? If it's a simple song you may find the answer in one of the pool and fountain kits at your garden store. These may be used as is, or modified to better suit the spirit of your garden. The pool itself can be as simple as a scooped out hollow in the ground, lined with plastic film. Clean sand or smooth washed stones can be used to line the pool to hold the plastic down and protect it from mechanical and sun damage. Recirculating pump, the proper fittings, fountain heads or rings, and plastic film are included in the kits.

Building your own fountain

If building your own is your pleasure, you may find yourself creatively involved in hydraulics, plumbing, some carpentry; and perhaps the art of the sculptor.

For a starter, realize that anything that will hold water can be used as a garden pool. The idea of using a portable box as a pool suggests seasonal use on terrace or patio. The rectangular box in pool number 2 is made with ¾-inch marine plywood, capped with 2 by 3-inch redwood. Such a pool, assembled with brass screws and epoxy glue, is likely to outlive the builder. To add light and sparkle to the water, finish the inside of the pool with an epoxy marine paint, available in blues and blue-greens.

Whether water splashes, gurgles or simply sits and drips depends on the type of outlet you use. Fine spray holes, drilled in a capped pipe will give effect; copper tubing pinched at the end will give a coarse or fine spray depending upon the pinching. Fine sprays give interesting visual effects but the sound is limited unless you combine spray and cascading water—as takes place in fountain number 4 where bowls catch the water and allow it to cascade into the pool.

Fountain pumps

Suitable recirculating pumps are available from 1/50 horsepower up. The smallest generally available, pumps between 100 and 200 gallons per hour, depending on the amount of lift between intake and outlet, and the constriction of the outlet jets. Small unit is more than sufficient for fountains similar to number 3 and 4 in photos on opposite page. A multiple jet fountain such as number 2 will require about 1/10 horsepower pump with a capacity of 500 gallons an hour.

Both submersible type pumps and pumps requiring separate housing are available. With a submersible pump, the pool is a unit complete unto itself plumbing is limited to attaching pump outlet to the fountain heads. A table fountain such as number 4 in the photographs opposite page may be operated from a pump concealed below the table or may be built with a base large and deep enough to hide a submersible pump.

When brass or copper tubing is used, the tools of the trade are: a small propane soldering-brazing torch, a small wheel-type pipe cutter, solder and epoxy cement.

Controlled splash... upward splash... Poured concrete or ceramic containers — any size, any number

flat splash...

Subdued splash... Skipping splash...

Movable wooden containers with self-contained pump & fountain

For children's play — hinged water gates to change the path of the water

There's noisy, erratic splashing as this pond of movable sculpture is pounded by water from above

Brass, copper, or ceramic plate

Brass dowel

"Feely" — seeping water coats these very slick concrete surfaces for a smooth touch

A slight slope and a ⅛" lip prevents your water sheet from returning beneath

water source

Half copper pipes or ceramic tiles so arranged for continuous water play

1. Faucet collector's dream. Tune sound-volume by turning faucets. *2.* Bowls were specially fired to receive ½-inch pipe. Pot saucers (drilled) or shallow flower pots could be used instead. *3.* Trickle of water drops through obstacle course encrusted on vase. *4.* Table fountain suggests a bouquet of copper and sparkling water. Copper cups are available at plumbing supply stores.

Sunlight...
it powers
the garden

From the beginning of time observant gardeners have been sun worshippers. They knew the laws of solar radiation and reradiation very well. Today's gardeners have more materials to work with in manipulating the environment of a plant but the old laws of radiation and reradiation give direction to the best use of the new materials.

Solar radiation—the sun is a gigantic fiery furnace 93 million miles away from us. Every second its tremendous energy bombards the earth with incredible force. The radiation it sends off heats whatever surface it hits, but not the air it travels through.

When the sun's rays reach the earth they are absorbed or reflected back depending on what kind of surface they hit. The rays that warm objects they hit are "short" rays. The object heated reradiates the stored heat but with a different wave length: the long rays. Heat stored in the soil is reradiated at night. The amount of heat stored in the soil depends upon the color of the soil, water in the soil, and the cover over the soil. A cover of light colored straw, for example, will reflect such a large portion of the short rays that the net input of incoming radiation is small. On the other hand, with black colored moist soil there is no reflection and the net incoming radiation is high.

In Florida where high soil temperatures are a problem, mulches are sometimes painted white to reflect the short rays and effectively lower soil temperatures.

The short rays of the sun travel through glass, translucent paper, clear plastic film, and plastic containers of all types, to heat the soil beneath and, through reradiation, the air above it. The hot cap of paper allows the short rays to penetrate the soil during the day but prevents or slows the escape of the long rays from the soil at night.

The nature of the soil cover you add as a mulch determines the input

◁

A mulch of bark chunks modifies the sun's power to heat soil to temperatures damaging to plants roots, and "dresses up" the garden.

of heat stored. The clear plastic mulch allows the short rays to enter the soil, but traps loss of heat, increasing soil temperatures by 10° or more. A thick layer of organic matter such as sawdust or similar material reduces the input of heat. A cover of reflective material such as aluminum foil or white coated plastic will reflect the short rays of the sun to drop soil temperature below that of soil which is directly exposed to the sun's rays.

Manufacturers and experiment stations are working with many new types of plastic mulches. Aluminum paper is now being used by some commercial growers; blue plastic has been used for the same aphid-repelling ability. Slitted clear plastic is being tested in commercial planting. However the home gardener has a most valuable gardening aid in the widely available clear and black polyethylene film.

Black plastic film. Black polyethylene has built itself a solid reputation for increasing yields and speeding up ripening of melons, eggplant, peppers and summer squash. In areas where early season temperatures are less than ideal for these warm weather crops, yields of muskmelon in experimental plots have been increased up to 4 times over that of non-mulched plants.

The increase in soil temperature is given credit for the remarkable speed-up of growth. However, temperature readings show that the increase is generally in the 3 to 6° range, sometimes only 2°.

The temperature of the film soars high on a warm sunny day and kicks back a great deal of heat to the air above it, rather than transferring it to the soil. Insulating air pockets, between the film and the soil surface, retards heat transfer from the black film to the soil.

Make sure that the soil is damp when the mulch is applied so that there is sufficient moisture under the mulch for the mulch to retain. Dry soil should not be mulched unless there is ample water available to soak the beds after mulching.

Subsequent watering through plastic mulches is not a problem and the advent of drip irrigation systems will make watering under mulches a water-saving operation. See pages 16-17 about drip irrigation. Users of plastic mulches now take care of water needs by cutting upside-down T-slits in the plastic when watering with sprinklers, or running water through the planting holes, or laying a soaker hose under the plastic or by penetration from the side of the mulched rows.

This small version of the A-frame was invented by a gardener intent upon increasing spring-time soil temperatures. Built with hinged sides, it can be picked up and stored when not needed. This portability, allowing use only at night is in its favor. Open ends allow circulation.

This gardener, harvesting his crop of strawberries planted in clear plastic mulch evidently knows his business and would not be using the plastic bottles (upper left in photograph) unless they gave him the protection he wanted in his climate.

In commercial plantings in San Diego County, California, clear plastic is used for windbreaks, soil mulch and row cover as the site and season demands. Above right: plastic jugs without bottoms are used like "hot caps"; stakes keep bottles

from blowing away. In cool weather, build up of heat is checked by air released through neck of bottle. Hot weather causes excessive heat build up inside jugs. Jugs should be removed on hot days.

Wire covered frame used to protect plantings from birds doubles as row tent with the addition of plastic cover over wire.

Stumbling blocks with plastic

Where such early-season growing aids as row covers and plastic bottle are used is all important. Where temperatures are consistently cool they fullfil their function very well. But where a stretch of cool spring weather may be broken by temperatures equal to a hot summer day, the gardener may find the plastic-covered plant cooked to death.

The pluses & minuses of mulches

Mulch	Chance in soil temperature	Performance
CLEAR PLASTIC	+10	Short rays of sun penetrate clear plastic and warm soil; plastic traps evaporating water. Increases early growth in cool season, also stimulates weed growth beneath plastic.
BLACK PLASTIC	+6	Short rays heat black plastic which in turn warm soil. Solves weed problem. Increases crop yields of many crops. Protects fruit of vine crops from rot. See text.
BROWN PAPER MULCH	as much as −8	Light brown paper mulch with thin plastic coating reflects most of the short rays from the sun. It's biodegradable. Soil temperatures are as much as 8° lower than first inches of exposed soil. No weeds.
ALUMINUM COATED PLASTIC & FOIL	as much as −10	Reflective surface bounces back short rays from the sun. Soil temperatures are as much as 10° cooler than top inches of exposed soil. Research findings show that reflective surfaces repel aphids.
ORGANIC MULCHES	as much as −10	Thick mulch of organic matter stops sun's rays before they hit the soil. Soil surface layer as much as 10 degrees cooler than exposed soil. Stops most annual weeds if applied thick enough. Needs yearly additions.

Soil thermometer and maximum-minimum thermometer with sunshield were used to measure effect of various plastic mulches and coverings. Below: To see if increase in early night temperatures would speed growth in early planting of peppers, a 4x8 foot fiber glass panel was arched over part of row at sunset each day, removed next morning. Soil and air temperatures, read at 11 p.m., were higher than those in open row. Plastic covered peppers grew faster, larger than those in open ground.

In the above chart we have compared the basic qualities of each type of mulch. Which is for you is not the question. You may use all types—each in its proper season and its need in your climate. You modify your climate when it is improved by the modification. A thick mulch applied *before* the soil has a chance to warm up is the worst thing you can do for plants in need of early warmth.

Experiment station report

The following letter from J. W. Courter gives a comparative picture of the use of plastics in the home garden. Courter is an Extension Specialist in Small Fruit and Vegetable Crops at the University of Illinois College of Agriculture and secretary of the National Association of Plastics in Agriculture. The letter reads:

"Plastics can be of great benefit to home gardeners to modify (hopefully improve it!) the environment in which plants are growing. This is accomplished by modifying soil temperature, conserving soil moisture, controlling weeds, preventing root injury due to close cultivation or hoeing, maintaining good soil structure by preventing crusting and compaction of the soil, reflection of light to repel insects, modify air temperatures for optimum growth, improve soil moisture holding capacity and provide economical means of water distribution (trickle irrigation). Then of course, plastics find many other uses as pots, flats, labels, bird control netting, etc.

"One of the real problems is educating the gardener on how a particular plastic acts (modifies) on the environment, which vegetable or crop plant will be benefited by that change, and how to use the material in question.

"Ordinary polyethylene film, available in rolls three or four feet wide and

1 to 1.5 mils thickness, makes an excellent mulch. It is true that clear film will warm the soil more than black film. Black film, however, prevents weeds from growing underneath because it excludes light needed for their growth. Therefore, we promote the use of black film rather than clear film for home gardens. The exception would be where we would want to promote early development of sweet corn or some other early seeded crop. We may or may not want to leave the film in place for the entire season depending on whether or not a chemical herbicide is used. This is a limitation for the home gardener.

"The use of clear polyethylene film also can be used to promote germination of early vegetables. I have seen it used very successfully for covering lettuce, radishes, and even early potatoes. The film is removed after the seedlings emerge from the soil. In the case of potatoes, slits may be cut to allow the plants to grow through the film. The home gardener may then leave the film in place and cover it with an organic mulch such as straw or even sawdust. Or the home gardener can make his own slit mulch for corn, beans, etc. So you can see that both clear and black may be used as long as the gardener understands the advantages and drawbacks of each.

"After the crop plant gains size and shades the mulch, the mulch has *less effect* on soil temperature. The warming or cooling effect of the mulch, I feel, has its greatest influence early in plant development. Later other factors such as uniform soil moisture, good aeration and less compaction of the soil, and possibly greater availability of nutrients become more important. Increased soil temperature is not enough to explain yield increases. In fact when all natural environmental conditions are near ideal some vegetables may not show response to mulch. For example, in some years deep-rooted vegetables such as tomatoes may show little benefit from mulching. In contrast shallow-rooted vegetables such as vine crops (cucumbers, etc.) show a response in most years. Use of mulches certainly can be justified for reasons other than yield increases."

Demonstration garden report

Duane Hatch, Extension Agent in Eugene, Oregon brings some of the Oregon State University's research findings to the gardening public through the "Hatch Patch" demonstration garden. One proof-of-the-pudding has been his experience with plastic mulches. He reports:

Top: the 1974 Plastic Garden at Dixon Springs Agricultural Center in Simpson, Illinois. Newly planted garden shows many kinds of vegetables growing in small space, mulched with black plastic. Above: the same garden a few weeks later. Note the areas between the rows are mulched with sawdust to keep down weeds.

Extension Agent, Duane Hatch, shown here in demonstration garden, proves clear plastic mulch will add extra warmth needed to ripen melon crops in western Oregon's cool summers (see text). Garden shown here with plastic mulched beds ready for planting.

23

"A layer of plastic over the soil aids greatly with warm season crops such as tomatoes, melons, peppers and squash. The warming of the soil will promote 10 to 14 days earlier maturity and higher yields with tomatoes. Melons, seeded about the 10th of June gave us ripe canteloupe and watermelon by mid-September.

"We demonstrated that clear plastic is better than black plastic because the sun's energy is expanded on the soil rather than on the top part of the plastic. The weeds were not a major problem under the clear plastic if temperatures of 90° or more occurred to burn off the weeds. In 1974 we aren't getting enough heat to burn off the weeds, and we have had to lift the plastic and do some hand weeding.

"The hills of squash and melons were planted through an X cut in the plastic. With the amount of water that goes through the planting hole and around the edge of the plastic, no special watering was necessary."

Mulching

Few actions in the vegetable or flower garden are so rewarding as mulching. Even the words "to mulch" suggest a nice thing to do to soil.

The mulches may be organic material such as leaves, peat moss, straw, manure, sawdust, ground bark, compost and the like; or a manufactured material like black plastic.

When you follow the best use of both, you join hands with the ancients and today's agricultural technologists.

The importance of organic mulches and combinations plastic/organic

Organic mulches. The plastic mulches may have great advantages in increasing crop yields and in weed control, but they in no way deny the value of organic mulch. Throughout the garden an organic mulch will benefit plant growth in many ways and at the same time give the garden a well-groomed look.

Remember that the values of organic mulches are summer-time values—reducing soil temperatures and water saving. The vegetable gardener especially should understand that.

Home garden experiment with mulches for strawberries using brick laid on sand and clear and black plastic mulch. Berries are watered by soaker hose beneath the plastic. As weather warmed and extra heat not needed, plastic was covered with bark mulch.

Paper mulch with a thin coating of polyethylene is now manufactured in 24 and 36-inch widths in rolls of 50 and 100 feet. Two colors offered: natural brown for summer; black for winter. As a summer mulch it reduces water evaporation, evens out soil temperatures, stops weed growth, prevents fruit rot and increases crop yield. In addition it's biodegradable. Laid over the soil, holes are cut for transplants or seeds.

An application of an organic mulch in early spring will slow up the natural warming of the soil as spring advances. As an insulating blanket it reduces solar radiation into the soil. As a result, frost hazards are greater with a mulched bed.

In the vegetable garden. If you find yourself going over the soil with a cultivator, after a rain or after watering, in order to break up the surface crust, then you need a mulch. Raindrops do a cementing job by packing the small particles between the larger ones so that the pores are plugged and neither water nor rain can enter. A mulch breaks the pressure of the water drops and pore space remains open.

Weed control. For weed control the organic mulch must be thick enough so that weed seedlings can't go through it on their own stored food. Perennial weeds will thrive in spite of organic mulches, or because of them. Black plastic will take care of all kinds of weeds and grasses and it can be used as a base for any of the organic mulches.

Conserves moisture. Mulches slow down the evaporation of water from the upper 6 to 8 inches of soil. Tests show that merely shading the bare soil will reduce evaporation as much as 30 percent, but a straw mulch will reduce evaporation as much as 70 percent.

A mulch not only saves water, but it helps maintain a more even moisture supply in the upper layers of the soil.

The richest layers. By insulating the top few inches of the soil from the sun's heat and maintaining soil moisture to the surface of the soil, a mulch gives the roots a free run in the richest layers of the soil. Tests show that plant roots under the mulch develop as extensive a deep root system as they do under bare soil. The surface roots are an added bonus.

Of course, if the lower layers of the soil are unfavorable to full root development such as with heavy clay that drains slowly, the plant will concentrate most to the roots near the surface of the soil.

In the vegetable garden, a mulch beneath unstaked tomatoes, summer squash, and cucumbers lessens the loss of fruit through rot. A tomato sitting on damp soil invites the soil bacteria to do their normal thing. Muddy splashes of rain may start rot in lettuce.

How thick a mulch? Apply organic mulches 1 to 2 inches thick for the fine materials such as sawdust. Coarse or fluffy materials can be applied 3 to

Mulches are layers of something over the soil—a layer of gravel, bark chunks, or of plastic film, or of any material the gardener chooses. The combination of plastic film overlaid with gravel or bark is the answer when a weed-free, no-maintenance area is wanted. The ''gravel gardens'' are less austere when beds of flowers or shrubs are arranged in them. Large rocks modify soil temperatures as any other mulch. They give a cool, moist root run to plants growing alongside of them.

4 inches thick. Materials such as straw or chopped corncobs may be covered with a more attractive mulch.

Untreated sawdust will cause some degree of nitrogen shortage. Soil bacteria go to work on the sawdust, and take their necessary supply of nitrogen from the soil. The loss is not as great as when sawdust is mixed in the soil. A good rule of thumb measurement is to increase the amount of fertilizer regularly used for the crop by ¼ when using a sawdust mulch.

Caution in applying. Apply mulch evenly. When using a mulch that becomes soggy when wet, don't pack it around the stem or trunk of the plant. When the mulch is thoroughly wet, pull it back a few inches from the stem or trunk so there is free air circulation to the base of the plant.

Gradually improves soil structure. Mulches should be maintained at the original thickness. As the mulch thins down, add new material. As the mulch decomposes or is washed into the soil the structure of the soil is gradually improved.

Combination mulching. The same gardener using plastic mulches for early spring soil warm-up doesn't need to worry if summer temperatures are too hot for plastic. Just add an organic mulch to cool the plastic. In the desert where summer temperatures of more than 100° are the rule, black plastic for weed control, covered with organic mulch such as bark, is a good growing combination for many shrubs.

Reflectors coffee cans and mulch

The problem: In the only space available for a planting of corn an 8 foot hedge stopped the morning sun; a 10 foot hedge put the garden in shade in late afternoon. In the first experiment aluminum foil was stapled to plastic and hung on both east and west sides of planted area. Corn crop was perfect except in rows next to hedge. The next year reflective panels of metalized plastic with adjustable angle of reflection were more efficient.

Nighttime warmth

We built a plastic A-frame and found a way to keep it warm on cold nights. We put large plastic bleach bottles full of water inside the A-frame. The sun warms the water during the day. At night it slowly gives off heat and keeps the A-frame several degrees warmer than the outside air.

Tomatoes and late frost

We extend our tomato season by as much as three weeks by laying a wide strip of black plastic over each row at night. This year we will do the same with peppers and eggplants.

Windburn, sunburn sometimes are crop stealers. Shingles protect plant (left). Protecting melon (right) when temperatures are high with wooden crate is one solution; some gardeners whitewash melons. USDA research has developed a spray of chemically inert aluminum silicate for use on melons to reflect sunlight and lower temperatures of the fruit.

Having frosts around September 20-30 we lose a lot of fruit unless we protect in this way.

Planting through plastic-film mulches

From a test garden at the University of Illinois—when setting transplants of vegetables such as tomatoes or peppers through mulch, we find it very easy to accomplish this using a small hand bulb planter. By sharpening (filing) the bottom edge it cuts through the mulch cleanly (with a twisting motion) and makes a planting hole in the soil beneath. This method is simple and avoids the unnecessary tearing of the mulch when a hole is made by hand. For *seeding* vegetables (beans, corn, etc.) through mulch, an old-fashioned corn planter (jabber) does a very nice job. You simply push the planter through the mulch and use it as you would in cultivated soil.

Coffee cans

I am sure you have many ideas already. Hotkaps I am not crazy about as they can blow away if not carefully anchored and they sometimes get the plant too hot. We have had good luck with respect to late light frosts with 2-pound coffee cans, both tops and bottoms removed. We put them over our tomatoes, eggplants, and peppers and leave them for a couple of weeks. Occasionally the tips of the leaves get burnt by the hot metal on contact, but the damage is not permanent. We also use on cabbage plants, not against frost but as protection against bugs. The advantage of the open-ended can is that you don't have to lift every morning and replace each night. Of course it's not protection against a heavy frost, but one would not normally be putting out tender plants that early.

Mulches in North Dakota

Tomato growing trials in a North Dakota experiment station were planned to determine whether organic mulches made the soil too cool even in July and August.

Soil temperatures, at 4 inch depth, were recorded to determine number of hours temperatures were below 58 degrees—the minimum for efficient growth.

In the period June 21-July 25 while air temperatures were below 58° for 122 hours and open ground soil temperatures for 70 hours, there were only 2 chilling hours under white plastic. August 5-19 the temperature comparisons were: Air 65 hours, soil 38 hours, plastic mulch 0 hours.

A black garden in Wayne, New Jersey

The story of this garden all began with a letter from Gus Gagis in Wayne, New Jersey. Gus readily admitted that he was a novice gardener, unfamiliar with the "art of gardening," but he became very intrigued with the idea of the black plastic mulch.

Gus had difficulty finding the recommended plastic (3 feet wide, 1½ mils thick) but he did come across a commercially available black plastic, 4 mils thick in a 10 x 25 foot size. He purchased two of these sheets and covered a 15 x 25 foot garden area with the plastic, "wall-to-wall," rather than just the rows as is normally recommended.

It was a little difficult for neighbors and other gardeners to accept this black, shiny surface as a vegetable garden. Gus reported, "I must admit that the sight of this 'black garden' evoked many wisecracks and skeptical comments from both family and friends alike, but I perservered." That was in the early stages; the plants grew so rapidly that the value of the black plastic soon became obvious, and the plastic itself *less* obvious.

Although Gus was a novice gardener, he was the type of novice that more seasoned gardeners respect. He started his gardening adventure with the latest information from test gardens everywhere. When choosing the seeds and plants for his garden Gus favored the hybrid varieties. He planted two types of cucumbers, 'Burpee hybrid' and 'Surecrop,' two varieties of summer squash, 'Greyzini' and 'Goldbar,' three varieties corn, 'Earliking,' 'Golden Cross Bantam' and 'Silver Queen,' and a mixture of ornamental gourds. From transplants he planted 'Samson' muskmelon, 'Black Beauty' eggplant, 'Calwonder' peppers, 'Dixie Queen' watermelon and two varieties of tomatoes, 'Early Spring Giant' and 'County Fair' hybrid.

Gus placed wire cages around the indeterminate tomatoes (Spring Giant). When he couldn't find the recommended 4 x 4 inch mesh concrete reinforcing wire, Gus settled for 2 x 4 inch mesh and snipped out alternate wire to make a 4 inch mesh.

In a few weeks time, the growth of the vegetables had nearly covered the plastic so that the soil temperature was doubly modified.

A dry spell started around the 9th of July and has lasted through the last report we had on July 23rd. The watering demand was not as great as it would have been in an open garden, and only required an occasional soaking by inserting a garden hose under the plastic and letting the water spread. Gus had taken advantage of previous rains with T-shaped slits in the plastic.

Since this was a first time garden for Gus Gagis there is no way to compare this year's crop with last years with regard to earliness or increase in yield, but he said, "when I compared notes with other home gardeners who were severe critics of my experiment initially, my yield to date far surpasses all of those I have spoken to. "And he seems to be the first one to carry his vegetable trophies in for those in the office. "And one thing's for sure," Gus told us, "not only my immediate family, but all my relatives really enjoy the extra bounty from the 'black garden.'

July 9th in Wayne, New Jersey

Time	Outside Temp. °F	2" Depth		4" Depth		6" Depth	
		Ground	Blk. Pls.	Ground	Blk. Pls.	Ground	Blk. Pls.
9:15 AM	74	68	77	—	—	62	68
10:00 AM	76	73	77	65	71	64	70
11:00 AM	80	77	80	71	75	65	71
1:00 PM	86	82	90	75	80	70	75
2:00 PM	90	86	93	79	88	73	79
6:00 PM	85	84	96	79	91	76	86
7:30 PM	82	81	91	79	90	75	86
9:00 PM	78	—	91	—	—	—	—

The photograph above shows an assortment of "shade" and "partial shade" in an area adjoining a patio.

Here, spreading its color beneath an early blooming magnolia the Fairy Primrose (Primula malacoides) proves its value in the landscape. It is equally rewarding, in the mild winter areas of California, for weather-proof winter container plantings. Used as a houseplant in cold winter sections.

Partial shade, light shade is welcomed by many plants when direct sunlight is intense and temperatures are high. Ferns and many colorful foliaged plants have their rightful place in the shade garden, but when you start looking for annuals or perennials that will add colorful bloom, the list of candidates grows short. In the chart at the right we list the popular color producers in the shade garden.

The list will become much longer if the "shade" garden is a "partial-shade" garden. Or if you don't object to a certain amount of legginess and sparse bloom. The gardener who makes a difference between shade-loving and shade-tolerant plants is the successful one. Most gardeners take the advice that such and such a plant does well in shade too literally. Generally, if the amount of sunlight is increased to the maximum the leaves will tolerate it and the plant will deliver maximum bloom. Equally true is the fact that the sun-produced bloom will last longer when protected from the direct sunlight. Remember, almost any plant will remain bushy and strong for weeks, and bloom its head off in the shade, if it is grown to full-bud stage in the sun.

Impatiens—new colors and forms for problem shade areas

When you talk about color in shady areas the most exciting plant today is

"Color in shade"

Name of plant	Type	Remarks
Begonia, fibrous rooted *Begonia semperflorens*	Perennial	Flowers in red, white, pink. Leaves are deep waxy green or bronzy red.
Begonia, tuberous rooted *Begonia tuberhybrida*	Bulb	Many new strains available. Long time favorites as summer pot plants and hanging baskets.
Coleus	Perennial grown as an annual	Prized for brilliantly colored leaves. Use outdoor in summer and as houseplant anytime. Color not as vivid in shade.
Fairy Primrose *Primura malacoides*	Annual	Tiers of tiny flowers in pink, rose, white and lavender. In mild climates blooms from Jan. to May. Plant in wide shallow pots.
Floss Flower *Ageratum Houstonianum*	Annual	Compact multi-branch plant 5-12 inches high. White, pink or blue flowers. An excellent dwarf variety is 'Blue Mink.'
Forget-me-not *Myosotis sylvatica*	Annual	Look for dwarf kinds. Brings shades of clear blue into the shade border.
Impatiens *Impatiens walleriana*	Perennial in milder areas of the west, used elsewhere as an annual	Bright scarlet, pink, orange, red, rose or white flowers 1 to 2 inches across. Dwarfs and semi-dwarfs are available.
Italian Bellflower *Campanula isophylla*	Perennial	Trails to 2 feet. Choice in hanging baskets late summer and fall.
Lobelia erinus	Annual	Use dwarf compact kinds for wide shallow pots and trailing type for hanging baskets.
Pansy *Viola tricolor hortensis*	Perennial grown as an annual	Use for winter and spring color in mild winter areas, spring and summer in cool climates.
Scarlet Sage *Salvia splendens*	Perennial	Often listed as plant for full sun but does well in semi-shade.
Wishbone Flower *Torenia fournieri*	Annual	Compact low growing. Full sun where summers are cool. Stamens arranged in shape of a wishbone.

the Impatiens. The wide range of colors, the willingness to bloom continuously, the versatility in use—ground cover, hanging basket, pot plant—are the virtues known to gardeners for years. But the new F1 Hybrids have widened the color range of straight color and bi-colors, and improved the growth habit of many dwarf types.

You don't know impatiens if you haven't been nursery shopping lately.

There's the Imp series with choice of pink, purple, orange, deep orange, rose, salmon, carmine, white and scarlet 2-inch flowers on many-branched 15-inch high plants.

The Elfin series is available in 8 colors. The plants are self-branching at the base with no pinching required. They are uniform in growth habit, and reach a height of 12 to 15 inches. Plants are covered with flowers through the season.

The Shadeglow series comes in solid and variegated colors. The solid variety comes in 8 colors and reaches a height of 10-inches; the variegated grows to 8-inches and has four different color combinations. Large and abundant blooms; plant is resistant to summer heat and unfavorable weather. 'Zig-Zag' rose and white has the same basic habit as the Shadeglow series and grows to 10-inches.

Stars and Stripes series. A white star sets off the scarlet, orange, pink

Indoors or out—ferns are naturals in the shade. They'll thrive with frequent mistings to increase humidity.

The colorful performance of the many flowered fibrous begonias and the dramatic tuberous-rooted begonia brighten tunnel-like areas of deep shade.

Hanging pots, boxes and baskets are easier to take care of when given alternate shade and sunlight as with a lath overhead or similar protection.

Pacific hybrids of the hardy polyanthus primrose offer 3-inch late winter flowers in a variety of clear colors.

and purple flowers of this variegated impatiens, and its bronze foliage makes a striking accent.

The impatiens buff is always looking for the sport, the variation in color of flower or leaf. The collector may find the prize in a mixed batch at a nursery or in a group grown from seed. Increasing the one prize plant to many plants is no trouble as impatien cuttings root quickly.

When growing impatiens from seed, remember that the seed is light responsive and germinates best if sown on the surface of the soil mix, covered with clear plastic or glass until the seed germinates.

Vegetables in the shade

Where there is no full-sun space the rule of thumb to use in locating vegetables in various spots around the house goes like this: All vegetables that are grown for their fruits or seeds such as, corn, tomatoes, squash, pumpkin, cucumbers, eggplant and peppers should have the priority on the sunniest spots.

Vegetables grown for their leaves or roots like, beets, cabbage, carrots, chives, kale, leeks, lettuce, mustard, green onions, parsley, radishes, Swiss chard and turnips are less demanding of total sunlight and can be grown in partial shade.

Sun-grown buds bloom in shade

Annuals and other plants that demand lots of sun to bloom are surprisingly generous in their ability to bloom in the shade *after* the flower buds have formed. Therefore we have found it advisable to grow many sun-loving annuals in pots and other containers to move into our shaded patio for long lasting color we wouldn't normally have. We have also found that the individual bloom is larger and the flowering prolonged when sun-loving plants are allowed to bloom in the shade.

Garden color—move it indoors before frosts are due

There are many plants that lead a double life as outdoor-indoor plants. After doing their spring and summer duty outdoors, various potted plants and hanging baskets can come inside to brighten the winter months.

We talked with Glenn Vincent of Park's Seed Company, in South Carolina, about the plants that can give indoor color after blooming outside in the summer months. Based on his personal experience as a gardener, here's what he told us:

Ageratum, especially the dwarf varieties, gets wide use in the garden as a border edging or potted plant. Prized for their pale blue flowers, Ageratum does well indoors, and makes a fine hospital plant—especially where hospitals are hesitant about "smelly type" plants such as marigolds and chrysanthemums.

Fibrous begonias are unsurpassed for potted plants and shady summer beds. The new F1 hybrids are more easily grown, produce more flowers and can be grown in full sun. Flowers in red, white and pink; leaves are deep waxy green or bronzy red. Some of the new hybrids have clusters of yellow stamens in the center of each flower which adds an extra sense of aliveness and an interesting color note. Good for inside winter color.

Achimenes is an attractive flowering pot plant with flat-ended trumpet shaped flowers, 1 to 3 inches across in pink, lavender, orchid and purple. They double not only as an outside plant for baskets, pots, edgings and ground covers, growing in afternoon sun to partial shade, but work equally well as an attractive indoor plant. It does, however, need a resting period from October or November to January. At this time it should be stored in a cool, dry place to allow the rhizomes to ripen.

Browallia blooms with bell like flowers, 1½ to 2 inches wide, in shades of blue and white. These shapely dwarf plants are easy to grow and bloom profusely in sun or partial shade. It is excellent for borders, beds or pots, growing only 8 to 10 inches high, forming round compact mounds of bloom with glossy emerald foliage. After blooming in the garden until frost, it may be potted and brought indoors for bloom all winter.

Caladiums have brilliantly colored arrow-shaped leaves that can liven up a partly shaded bed, border or pot. They have no enemies and grow in any rich soil. When grown outdoors their magnificent leaves create a beautiful effect throughout the summer and fall. The Caladium can be grown indoors as a pot plant not requiring much light, only moisture, warmth and an occasional remark of admiration. Unfortunately, they do require a brief dormant rest period in mid-winter.

Balsam comes in a great many colors. The flowers are large and double in form, looking like a small camellia. Outside, Balsam does well planted in beds and borders, thriving in shade in any rich soil, and does well in pots also. If started in autumn, they will bloom inside in a window throughout the winter.

Coleus is one of the most colorful foliage plants for shady gardens, containers and planter boxes. It's great as a year-round houseplant, and can be easily rooted in water or in moist soil from cuttings. The luxuriant foliage is beautiful winter and summer and will display red, green, crimson, yellow, pink and combinations of these colors.

Impatiens, which of course you know, are my favorites for the shade. They come in many shades of pink, orange and white and bloom profusely all through the summer. They are excellent pot and hanging basket plants, and after performing all summer can be cut back and brought into the house for winter color.

Indoor Lettuce

From an apartment dweller: I found that 'Ruby' lettuce makes a beautiful house plant. I plant it in an 8 inch centerpiece bowl, keep it near a window well-watered and fertilized, harvest a salad about once every three weeks all winter.

Plants on the move

During the warmer months many houseplants benefit from a stay outside the house. It gives the gardener a chance to give the plants a light shower to wash off dust and grease that may have accumulated over the winter months. House plants should never be moved from inside the house into direct sunlight outside. If you are putting your house plants outside for a while, place them in a partially shaded area for a week, gradually moving them into a brighter location.

If you are moving outdoor plants inside for the winter, you will probably notice a period of a week or so when the plant does not look its best. Don't worry, the plant is just adjusting to its new environment. After a couple of weeks the plant may have lost some of its leaves or flowers, but they will be replaced when the plant has adjusted to its indoor climate.

From a nurseryman

Don't try to push the old reliables too far—each year I hear the complaint of petunias, marigolds, zinnias and others 'reaching for the sky' becoming pale, puny and susceptible to every hungry insect in the neighborhood. If you have a shaded area, choose a variety suited for that location—both the plants and the gardener will do better.

When there is no sunlight—in basement, living room or office—the garden under lights takes on many forms and functions. Whether individually designed or bought as a unit, these grow light assemblies are almost essential in starting seeds.

Baskets of impatiens in many colors hang like ornaments from tree branches. With its many forms, the impatiens play many roles in shady areas of the garden— as a border plant, a ground cover, as a pot plant or in hanging baskets.

These plants were selected for a high-rise Manhattan apartment which receives only filtered sunlight. In addition to shade tolerant tropicals, the city gardener adds seasonal blooming and sun-loving species from his fluorescent garden to enjoy for brief periods.

Sometimes the attention given plants is too "painstaking." There's a lot to be said for the wisdom of approaching vegetable gardening with a loss-expected attitude. As long as the gains exceed the losses you're a winner.

We like the attitude of one of our friends from Indiana to be noted by this letter to us: "We had very little production from the Baby Lima planting probably due to some small insect. We lost all of our cucumber plants either to mosaic or insects. Had great success with our succession plantings. Followed early plantings with late plantings. Beans and corn followed early plantings of peas. Had great success with beans, tomatoes, beets, broccoli, second planting of cucumbers, peppers, spinach, carrots and flowers. You would be surprised at how much we saved on groceries."

So they lost a crop of cucumbers.

We have the feeling that we shouldn't expect normal behavior in the vegetable garden. When we read the seed catalogs and come upon the words "crop failure" stamped across the description of the super-colossal item we were about to order, we know that we are not alone.

When we make a tour of the garden and see tomatoes volunteering their bounty in the strangest places and cabbage roots on the compost heap refusing to die, we wonder why we are expected to treat them with awe and respect. But when our first radish crop, of all things, is a complete failure, we know why we keep on writing.

We have learned something about the peculiar ways of cucumber, even know that the bean tendril twists counter-clockwise and that potatoes can be picked rather than dug. But first about tomatoes.

You don't have to have a garden to grow tomatoes. Tomatoes are ideal container plants. Dwarf varieties can be grown in 8-inch pots. Giant-sized plants will thrive in containers holding only 2 gallons of soil if you compensate for the limited root space by frequent watering and fertilizing.

Few plants are as adaptable to training as the tomato. Several varieties can be grown in hanging baskets. Others can be trained as an informal espalier on a trellis. We have grown them in plastic bags, planter boxes, baskets, plastic pails, wire cylinders lined with plastic. We have trained them on stakes and allowed them to train themselves in wire cages.

No fruit-producing plant in the vegetable garden has greater willingness to grow. But there are some pitfalls.

Tomatoes... Guidelines for the unwary

- Know the habits of the plant
- Mulch or train the plant to hold fruit above ground
- Choose the right variety for your climate
- Favor disease resistant varieties
- Remember that it's a warm weather plant

The more you know about the growth habits of the tomato the easier it is to cope with its sometimes peculiar behavior.

The tomato is rather particular about air temperatures—especially night temperatures. In early spring when day temperatures are pleasantly warm but night temperatures fall below 55°, many tomato varieties will bloom but not set fruit. The blossoms drop off before they are fertilized. However most of the early maturing varieties set fruit at lower temperatures than the main season varieties.

Rain or prolonged humid conditions hamper fruit set. Growers in cool, humid situations have found that fruit set can be increased by shaking the plant, or vibrating it with a battery-powered vibrator (your electric toothbrush is a good substitute). When plants are trained on stakes, hitting the top of the stakes will increase pollination by releasing pollen. Best time to shake the plants is in midday when it's warm and the humidity is low.

Color and temperatures

When the temperature is above 86° and there is high light intensity,

Transplants should be stocky—not leggy—with 4 to 6 true leaves, young and succulent.

the red color will not form in fruit exposed to direct sun. The fruits may sun scald. Where high summer temperatures are the rule, choose varieties with a good dense foliage cover.

All vine and no fruit

The tomato plant sometimes fails to change gears from the leaf producing stage to the fruiting stage of growth. Given a strong push in the early stages with too much nitrogen and all the water it can use, it may go right on producing foliage at the expense of fruit. You can help the plant switch over to the fruiting stage by pinching out some of the terminal shoots, or by withholding water to check growth, or even by root pruning.

When leaves curl

Another worrisome period in your life with a tomato is the appearance of curled leaves or some form of wilt.

During a hot spell, at midday, wilt is normal. Plants in containers show the need for water by their wilting and drooping of top growth.

Some kinds of leaf curl are normal. It's more pronounced in some varieties than others. Expect curl during hot dry spells and during and after a long wet period. Heavy pruning seems to encourage leaf curl.

Feeding schedule

The tomato plant has a lot of work to do. An early variety is expected to produce a crop in about 60 days from the time the young plant is set out.

A vigorous main season variety will start producing in 70 days, continue production until cut down by frost.

The soil in which they are planted should have a good supply of nutrients—especially phosphorus. Before planting mix fertilizer into planting hole at rate on the label. After planting,

◁

Tomatoes hanging from the eaves outside the family room window.

Tomatoes luxuriate in half whiskey barrel, with 3 stakes for support.

Trellis training is one of easiest methods. Here pot grown plant was trained after plant developed.

"Small Fry" in planter box tied to vertical frame of 1 by 2-inch lumber.

no additional feeding is neccesary until fruit is set. Then feed plants monthly.

When you set out a transplant use a starting solution such as Ortho Tomato Food 6-18-6.

Watering

In the early stages of growth, before fruit has set, it is a good idea to put the plant under slight stress by stretching the interval between waterings.

After fruit has set it's important to maintain an even soil moisture. Fluctuating wet and dry spells is one way to bring on stunting of plants and blossom-end rot.

Blossom-end rot

Symptoms of this disease appear as a leathery scar or rot on the blossom end of fruits. It can occur at any stage of development. It is usually caused by sudden changes in moisture in the soil. Lack of calcium in the plant is another cause of blossom-end rot.

Remember, it's a warm-weather plant

You gain nothing by setting out transplants before the weather warms. Transplants set out too early just sit and sulk unless given special protection from cold night temperatures.

Wire cages

Gardeners have worked out dozens and dozens of ways to train plants so that the fruits are up off the ground.

Probably the favorite way to train large growing tomatoes is the circular cage made from concrete reinforcing wire. The 6-inch mesh allows for easy picking within the cage. No pruning is necessary. Yield of quality fruit will be higher in cages than on stakes. (See illustration)

Early production

Training to a stake with all of the suckers removed is the way to get fruit early. However the single stem method cuts down total production and in hot weather the fruit of the heavily pruned plant may be damaged by sun scald. However if you allow 1 or 2 suckers to grow from near the base and to form a 2 or 3 stemmed

Support for tomato plants

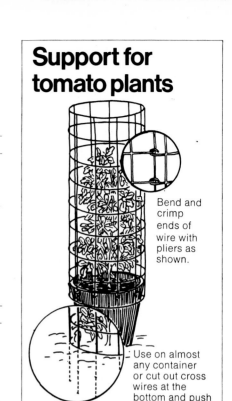

Bend and crimp ends of wire with pliers as shown.

Use on almost any container or cut out cross wires at the bottom and push into the ground.

A cylinder of 6" mesh concrete reinforcing wire makes an ideal support. Keep branches inside wire until they reach the top.

Wrap plastic around wire for protection.

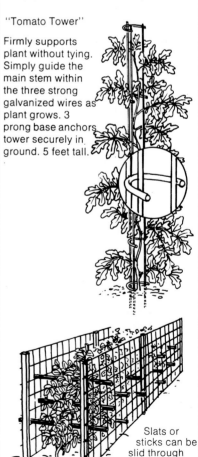

"Tomato Tower"

Firmly supports plant without tying. Simply guide the main stem within the three strong galvanized wires as plant grows. 3 prong base anchors tower securely in ground. 5 feet tall.

Slats or sticks can be slid through wire fencing on each side of your plants to give support when and where needed without tying.

plant you'll get more tomatoes with better foliage protection.

In our garden this year we tried the newly available Tomato Tower (see illustration). This stake of wires guides and holds the stem as it grows—requiring a minimum of tying.

Black plastic mulch

Gardeners with plenty of garden space find that a mulch of black plastic film under the vines allowed to sprawl naturally, not only keeps the fruits clean but increases yields. Strong growing varieties should be given a space of 3 by 5 feet when grown on plastic. See page 23 about black plastic.

Setting transplants

Set tomato plants deep—up to the first set of leaves, if they are leggy. If planting in peat pots be sure the rim of the pot is below soil level to prevent quick drying out.

Don't set a plant growing in a light soil mix in a small hole in heavy soil. Blend organic matter in a larger planting hole so that there is no abrupt change in soil texture.

Especially for containers

There are a number of varieties suitable for containers and hanging baskets. The smallest is 'Tiny Tim,' a 12-inch plant with cherry-sized fruits. The next in fruit size is 'Small Fry' with 1-inch fruits. However, 'Small Fry' is a vigorous grower to 30 inches and should be staked or used in a hanging basket. It produces hundreds of fruit—8 to 10 in a cluster. 'Burpee Pixie Hybrid' grows 18 inches tall with clusters of 1¾-inch fruit. 'Presto Hybrid' is about 24 inches tall with high quality 1½-inch fruit. 'Patio Hybrid' is a step larger, growing to a sturdy, compact 30 inches with 2-inch fruit.

All except 'Patio Hybrid' are in scale with a 6 to 8-inch pot. All bear quickly—50 to 55 days—and can be grown indoors as well as out. Give 'Patio Hybrid' a 12-inch or larger pot or plant it in the ground.

Varieties

In the list of varieties below, their disease resistance is indicated by the initials "V"—Verticillium, "F"—Fusarium, "N"—Nematode.

The number of days indicates the approximate time from setting out transplants to harvest.

The growth habit of the variety is

indicated by the words "determinate" and "indeterminate." (In text as "Det." and "Ind."). The determinates are the self-topping bush type, generally 3 feet or less. The indeterminates are the tall growers and are generally grown on stakes or trellis.

'Burpee Big Early' (62). Ind. Good size fruit.

'New Yorker' (64). (V.) Compact plant. Medium sized fruit. Mild flavor.

'Springset' (67). (V.F.) Det. Open growth habit.

'Willamette' (67). Det. Crack resistant. Low grower. Firm fleshed fruit. Does well in the Northwest.

'Better Boy' (72). (V.F.N.) Vigorous tall grower.

'Early Pak 7' (81). Det. Medium size deep firm fruit.

'Ace 55' (88) (V.F.) Det. Vigorous grower. Large smooth fruit.

'Pearson Improved' (90). (V.) Det. Medium large fruit.

Lettuce— For success with many vegetables know your way with this one

As with many vegetables these points are important in growing lettuce:

✔ Know what slices of the growing season it can fit into.

✔ Plant in small quantities in succession to avoid the glut of too much lettuce at one time.

✔ Don't ignore the advice on thinning.

✔ Know the types of lettuce.

✔ Know the difference between fertilizing for short-season and long-season crops.

✔ Know how to stretch the harvest season.

Lettuce is a cool season vegetable. The longer days and warmer nights of summer encourage flowering—"bolting to seed." By carefully choosing slow bolting varieties you may bring some lettuce through the summer.

Extend the harvest by a succession of small plantings. If sunlight in your garden is clear-sky intense sunlight,

Tomato trained teepee fashion in "all-seasons" fruit gardens at Los Angeles State and County Arboretum.

One way to keep tomatoes off the ground. Slats are placed to support fruit as they develop.

Low growing tomatoes in short cage have better protection from sun than if allowed to sprawl.

plant the summer lettuce in partial shade.

A little protection will stretch harvests months beyond the normal season.

HOW TO GROW. Buy transplants at your garden store, or grow your own transplants indoors. See page 86, about seed sowing and thinning. The final distance between plants is important with both head lettuce and leaf lettuce. Head lettuce needs 12-14 inches between plants. The thinnings can be transplanted for a somewhat later harvest. Leaf lettuce should be thinned twice. Eat the thinnings as you thin; first to 4-6 inches between plants, then 6-10 inches, depending upon the size of the variety.

Lettuce has a limited root system, and it occupies the soil for a relatively short time. Therefore, the importance of fertilizing and watering. If the growth of a young plant is checked by lack of nutrients or water, it never fully recovers. For best growth, add fertilizers to the soil *before* planting.

Never let the plant suffer from lack of moisture. The most critical period of water need is when the heads begin to develop.

It's perishable! Lettuce can't be frozen, canned or stored. Watch the number you plant at one time, but plant often to keep it coming.

Thinning. Most gardeners find it difficult to be ruthless in thinning any vegetable, but with lettuce they rationalize their reluctance with the thought that they will eat the leaves as the plants grow.

Actually, when you leave two plants of head lettuce in the space where only one should grow, all you get is two poor heads or no heads at all.

Some open leaf lettuce varieties can be harvested a leaf at a time, but with most the best part is the tender light green material in the center of the

almost mature plant. If you leave the row crowded with plants all you get is a bunch of little bitter outside leaves.

The 4 types of lettuce

There are 4 types of lettuce and dozens of varieties. The trick is to choose the variety that fits the season in your locality. In the following example of types, we mention only the varieties most frequently recommended.

Crisphead. Also known as Cabbage-head and Iceberg. If there is only one lettuce in the produce display, this will be it. More exacting in requirements than leaf lettuce, but is not at all impossible. Choice of the right variety is important, and 'Great Lakes' and 'Ithaca' are representative of this class and are widely recommended.

Butterhead. A heading type in which the leaves are loosely folded. Outer leaves may be green or brownish. Inner leaves are cream or butter colored. Butterhead types are not favored commercially because they bruise and tear easily. It's no problem in the home garden.

Representative and choice varieties 'Summer Bibb,' and 'Buttercrunch.'

Leaf Lettuce. More or less open in growth, leaves are thinner than the butterheads. Many variations in outer leaves; some frilled and crumpled, some deeply lobed. Leaf color varies from light green to red and brownish red.

'Grand Rapids' and 'Prizehead' or 'Bronzeleaf' are recommended early varieties, 'Slobolt,' 'Salad Bowl,' and

'Green Ice' are more heat resistant varieties.

Cos or Romaine. Grows upright 8 inches tall with tightly folded leaves. Medium green outer leaves and greenish white interior.

'Dark Green Cos' and 'Paris Island Cos' are widely adapted and available.

Varieties

The successful lettuce grower is choosey about the varieties he plants —both for the differences in quality and their special seasonal performance.

Crisphead class. "Great Lakes" (82-90 days). Crisp, serrated leaves, slow to bolt. May be bitter in hot weather. Used as a fall and winter crop in mild winter areas.

"Ithaca" (72 days). Mild, non-bolting and tipburn resistant variety for all seasons. Try spring and summer. May break down in late fall weather. "Fulton" is similar to "Ithaca."

"Imperial 44 and 456" (84 days). Heads are medium to small. For spring and summer growing.

"Penn lake" (70 days). Large and tender heads. Best in spring.

Butterhead class. "Dark green Boston" (73-80 days). Smooth, thick substantial leaves fold to form a loose head.

"Summer Bibb" (77 days). Small dark green leaves loosely folded. Has the quality of "Bibb" but is slow to bolt.

"Butter Crunch" (75 days). A large edition of "Summer Bibb" with thick leaves, more vigorous growth. Heat resistant and slow to bolt.

"Tom Thumb" (65 days). A miniature butterhead. Try it indoors.

Leaf lettuce or bunching. "Salad Bowl" (40 days). Crinkly tender leaves in a broad clump. Heat resistant and slow to bolt.

"Prizehead" or "Bronzeleaf" (45 days). Large, broad bronze-tinted leaves. Mild flavor; vigorous.

"Grand Rapids" (45 days). Light green leaves frilled and crinkled.

"Slobolt" (45 days). A "Grand Rapids" type that will stand more heat.

"Ruby" (50 days). Give it high marks for color.

"Green Ice" (45 days). Savoyed leaves with wavy and fringed leaf margin. Slow to bolt.

"Oakleaf" (40 days). A tight rosette of medium green, deep lobed leaves. Heat resistant; slow to bolt.

The lettuce box

With the idea that he could bring lettuce to the kitchen almost every month in the year, a gardener friend of ours built a 3-foot wide, 8-foot long cold frame, hot bed for lettuce growing only. He gave his earliest crops full sun or rain protection when needed. Summer crops received shade from the direct sun. Fall crops were protected from splashing rain when necessary and boosted along with the heat supplied with electric heating cables in the soil.

Cucumbers... They have some tricky growing habits

- Some have good disease resistance; some have not.
- Sometimes there'll be bitter cucumbers and no one knows why. New varieties are safer bets.
- One old, overripe cucumber, forming hard seeds will stop production of new fruits.

The home gardener should give the plant breeders and the seed producers a big hand for what they have done with cucumber varieties. Today the disease resistant varieties allow successful production in areas where diseases cut short the crop. The new hybrid varieties are more vigorous than the old and with most there is less chance of bitterness in the harvest.

So the choice of varieties becomes as important as how to grow them.

Varieties that are disease resistant:

Disease resistance may be an essential factor to look for. There are localities where many cucumbers can be grown with little attention to disease problems. There are places where scab, mosaic, powdery mildew, downy mildew, and anthracnose will put an end to your hopes for a crop. If you have had trouble growing cucumbers—and many gardeners "can't grow cucumbers"—try a disease resistant variety.

Listed below are some of the disease resistant varieties. Resistance or tolerance is indicated as follows: Scab (S), Mosaic (M), Downy Mildew (DM), Powdery Mildew (PM), Anthracnose (A). Hybrids are indicated by (H) following variety name. The name of the Experiment Station that developed the variety is included. Gynoecious hybrids (Gyn.) are all or nearly all female, produce fruits on the early flowers, usually have about 12% normal plants mixed in for pollination.

'Gemini Hybrid.' (H), (Gyn.), (DM), (M), (PM), (A), (S).

'Burpee Hybrid.' (M), (DM).

'Ashley.' Clemson (DM).

'Marketer.' (H), (DM), (M).

'Marketmore' (S), (M).

'Spartan Valor.' (Gyn.), (M), (S).

'Sweet Slice' (H), (M).

'Saticoy.' (H), (M), (D).

Picklers: Many varieties available. These have the advantage of disease resistance:

'Pioneer.' (H), (Gyn.), (S), (M), (DM), (PM).

'SMR 58.' (S), (M).

'SMR 18.' (S), (M).

'Ohio MR 17.' (M).

Flowers, then fruit

Don't worry about the failure of the first early flowers to set fruit. The male flowers open first, then about a week later you'll see flowers with baby cucumbers at their bases. The male flowers supply the pollen which is transferred by insects to the female flowers.

If this delayed setting worries you, try one of the new all-female (gynoecious) hybrids. They set fruit with the first blossoms and thus bear fruit closer to the base of the plant.

Cucumbers come in a wide variety of shapes and colors. There's a white one available—'White Wonder.' The low-acid 'Lemon Cucumber' is the size and shape of a lemon and at maturity turns a lemon yellow and then

Slow bolting types of 'Bibb' are 'Summer Bibb' and the prize winner, 'Buttercrunch.'

Of the varieties of leaf lettuce, 'Salad Bowl' is receiving top marks in the garden and the kitchen.

Varying in form and color, lettuce has a way of finding special places in any garden.

Raised beds frame a "show-off" planting of various kinds of lettuce. Leeks in the foreground.

a golden yellow. This old timer is easy to grow, always sweet and as burpless as any we have grown.

The very long, narrow cucumber you see in the produce markets is the English type, seedless when grown in greenhouses without pollination. Similar looking—long and slim are 'China Long' and 'China Hybrid.'

'Burpless Hybrid,' (60 days) is an excellent producer of 8-10 inch long fruits, 30 to 40 per plant. Mild and nearly seedless.

Special soil?

Cucumbers respond to generous amounts of organic matter in the soil. For special treatment, dig the planting furrow 2 feet deep and fill the first foot or so with manure mixed with peat moss, compost, sawdust, or other organic material. Fill rest of the furrow with soil, peat moss, and 5-10-10 fertilizer at the rate of 2 pounds to 50 feet of row.

Watering

If the plant is under stress from lack of moisture at any time it just stops growing. It will pick up again when moisture is supplied. It is normal for leaves of cucumbers to wilt in the middle of the day during hot spells, but check the soil for moisture at the below surface levels.

Training

Cucumbers trained on a trellis take very little ground space and you will harvest more attractive fruits and fewer culls. Cucumbers that are curved when grown on the ground, such as "Burpees Hybrid," grow almost straight when trained on a trellis.

Consider the midget varieties when space is limited. They can be grown on the ground, in tubs and boxes or as hanging baskets. Two such varieties are:

'Tiny Dill Cuke.' 55 days. Vines spread only 2 feet. Produces near finger-length cukes. University of New Hampshire development.

'Patio Pik.' 60 days. Vine is very dwarf, spreading only 18 to 24 inches. Pick small for dills, larger for slicing. Up to 7 inches long.

Very important

Keep all fruit picked from the vines as they reach usable size. The importance of this can't be overstressed, because even one fruit left to mature on the plant will completely stop the set of new fruit.

The correct way to pick a cucumber is to turn the fruit parallel to the vine and snap it sharply.

The root-crops... Many rewards some failures

Give deep soil to the deep rooted varieties.

Treat for soil insects before or as you plant.

Thin to give them root space and top space.

From tomatoes to lettuce to cucumbers we have followed the salad route. To be consistent, the vegetables to be considered next should be salad related. Naturally, it seems to us, in this classification are the carrot, radish, turnip, kohlrabi, and green onion. Each of these can be enjoyed in its raw state as well as in many other ways including salad making.

The method of growing each comes naturally to most gardeners and little trouble is expected in their growing. Our inclusion of kohlrabi in this group may have to be defended from critics who have never tasted it. It is excellent raw when simply chilled and sliced. As a variation the slices may be marinated in a French dressing. Crisp in texture, its flavor recalls that of both turnips and cabbage.

Salsify and Parsnips

Give the long season root crops— carrots, salisify, parsnips—a special soil and a special place.

In a raised bed, prepare a 12-inch deep soil mix with plenty of organic matter. Mix should be friable, fast draining and free of clods and rocks. Locate at edge or corner of garden so as not to interfere with succession planting of other crops.

Carrots

It's the vegetable you'll probably use most often, over the longest period of time. It's the vegetable of many uses, ranging from appetizers to desserts. It's not a vegetable to plant for the "home-grown" superiority to the carrots in the supermarket— the commercial grower will generally surpass the home gardener in the

production of quality and uniformity. But there's something just right about pulling a carrot, crisp and brittle (better water deeply first, or the tops will break off) washed clean with the hose, and munching on it as you survey your 10 foot garden.

HOW TO GROW. Carrot seed is planted ¼ to ½ inch deep, and takes from 10 to 17 days to germinate. The seed should never dry out. That means that you are expected to keep the top ¼ to ½ inch of soil moist for 2 to 3 weeks. Considering the soil may dry out in an hour or so when sun and wind combine their efforts, this seems as much of a chance as germinating seeds of the finest grass in the summer months.

In addition to the danger of drying out, there is the possibility of the soil forming a hard crust that not only prevents the sprouting seed from breaking through, but sheds water like a duck's back.

Gardeners have worked out several methods to prevent crusting over and drying out of the soil surface. One of the best ways to cover the seed row is with a thin mulch of vermiculite, bark or sawdust. If windy weather is expected, it's a good idea to contain the mulch in a slot to prevent it from blowing away.

A film of clear plastic over the seed bed will speed up germination by warming the soil, prevent crusting, and keep the soil moist. If weeds are a problem, they will be more so when clear plastic covers the soil. Keep a close watch for the emergence of the seedlings. Plastic must be removed as soon as seedlings show.

Consider sowing seeds of carrots in 4 or 6 inch bands, rather than in single rows. The problem of the first thinning is not as critical. There is less chance of tangled, malformed roots if the same number of seeds you normally sow in a foot of row are spaced out 4 to 6 inches wide. Some thinning will be necessary, but much of it will be in pulling baby carrots. The only disadvantage of the wide row is the necessity of more hand weeding than when planted in narrow rows.

Soil for carrots should be special. A box, 10 to 12 inches deep, and twice as wide, filled with light planter mix will deliver a good crop of straight, beautiful carrots. Regardless of whether in a box, raised bed, or at ground level, the soil must be free of rocks and clods for the roots to be straight and well formed.

For a long harvest of carrots in that half-grown size, make 3 sowings. The first in early spring, again when the first sowing is up and growing, and then in July for harvesting in the fall months.

Choose carrot varieties according to your soil and your preference for shape and size. The short-to-medium are better adapted to heavy or rough soils than the long types, and are easier to dig.

Short-to-medium—good for heavy soil and holds up well in wet fall and winter soils. 'Red Cored Chantenay,' 5½ inches long, heavy, stump rooted, widely adapted. 'Royal Chantenay' is a slightly longer, improved strain.

Long and slender—These 8 to 9 inch long varieties must have deep loose soil. Best in light sandy soil. 'Nantes;' good quality, tends to crack in wet fall weather. 'Imperator' is the standard market variety. 8½ inches long; good quality, widely adapted mid-season variety. 'Gold Pak,' deep orange color, small core.

Very short—good for heavy soils. Plump and short. 'Nugget,' resembles a radish, more than a carrot in shape. A round ball only 1-inch in diameter. Excellent quality.

Radishes

A very charming 4 year old girl sauntered through our garden with a packet of radish seed and planted, in the flower border, shrub border, planter boxes and pots, a seed or two. We harvested and ate some of her bountiful crops.

Why our ground plantings were riddled with maggots and her's were clean we'll never know—perhaps the cabbage maggot had not moved into our pots and planter boxes yet. We made some changes in our radish department since this failure.

No seed of radishes goes into the ground without protection from these destroyers. As soon as we have seeded a row we dust the furrow with Diazinon soil and foliage dust. This mild treatment kills the maggots as they hatch.

Although it seems reasonable that this fast growing crop should have a good supply of fertilizer to start with, we have dropped the amount in our garden to near zero. We were growing great tops and that was all.

Checking we found that, when well grown, the radish starts to bulb in about 2 weeks after sowing seed. So we paid more attention to thinning.

To avoid some of the thinning, we now plant radishes in wide bands as our carrots are planted. Perhaps we will try the "seed tapes" offered by several seed companies. Spend 85¢ for 16 feet of tape holding 192 seeds?

Tomatoes are training on wires suspended from overhead by a trapeze wire held by two poles.

When it comes to pole beans methods of training are very much as the gardener adapts and invents.

Here pole beans are trained on stakes placed in random patterns, another of many possible methods to try.

Tall growing peas attach themselves to long-lasting plastic netting stretched between supporting poles.

A cucumber that resented being caged within the wire trellis. Cucumbers grow straighter when hanging from the vine as freely as possible. See art, page 34, for type of cage.

Large cucumbers hang gracefully from an A-frame wooden trellis. They take little more ground space and produce more attractive fruits when trained this way. You easily see when they're ready to pick.

That's one seed per inch and if all come up that's 192 radishes. The prudent way to plant is to cut the 16-foot tape into 1 and 2-foot pieces and find spots around the garden to tuck them in—one at a time. There will probably be an accent on early spring planting and again in the fall.

Turnips

The turnip has virtues you may have overlooked. Realize that the turnip is borne partly out of the ground. No deep soil preparation is necessary. The seeds germinate quickly, and there's no special seedbed preparation. New hybrids have been introduced that produce small, good-eating turnips in 35 to 40 days.

Two factors in their growing need attention. First, treat as a fast growing crop. Never let them lack for water. Secondly, plant them as other cool crops, so that they mature in cool weather. This will be in very early spring or fall and winter, depending on your climate. (With a 35-day growing season you can afford to do a little experimenting.)

Our favorite variety for in-the-garden eating is 'Tokyo Cross.' This F1 Hybrid and All-American selection winner, lives up to its catalog description. The smooth, pure white, globe-shaped roots will grow to 2 inches in 35 days; will double that size without becoming pithy if allowed to grow. We planted small quantities both early and late without trouble from bolting.

Kohlrabi

It looks like a turnip above ground with leaves sprouting from all sides.

It's a short season crop, growing from seed to harvest in 55-60 days. Cultures as turnips. Plant for successive harvests for both spring and fall.

Remember, harvest kohlrabi *before* they are mature. Bulbs should be no more than 2 inches in diameter.

Potato piece planted at soil level forms roots below, and potatoes above soil. Mound with straw, peat

Woody stem fibers develop through the edible portion when fully developed.

Green onions

Any variety of the standard onion can be used as a green onion, if it is harvested when the bulb is small. Commercially, the green onion is always from a white variety. The home gardener generally grows green onions from "sets"—the small, dry onions available everywhere in late winter and early spring. Of the sets, the variety 'Ebenezer' are generally the yellow ones. 'White Lisbon' is the most widely grown for green-bunch onion sets.

In addition to the bulbing type of green onions, there are several perennial bunching types that continue to divide at the base to form new shoots throughout the growing season. They do not produce bulbs. In this group are such varieties as 'Beltsville Bunching,' 'Hardy White Bunching,' 'Japanese White Bunching,' 'Evergreen Bunching (Nebuka).' All are winter hardy and produce green onions throughout the growing season. Shoots are crisp and mild early in the season, more pungent later in the season. The term "scallions" is used loosely to describe several kinds of onions, but mostly applied to the non-bulbing onion.

Egyptian onions planted in early spring produces first, a delicious green onion bulb. If allowed to grow, the ripening stalk produces clusters of small, red bulblets. These mild flavored, small onions are excellent for pickling. The hollow stalks are ideal for stuffing. Production of bulblets may take place the first or second year.

Leeks

In appearance leeks look like a fattened green onion, with much larger top leaves and practically no swelling of the bulb. However, this hardy

moss, or other organic material instead of soil and you can pick potatoes instead of digging them.

member of the onion family has a delicate mild flavor in contrast to the onion. It's a fall and winter substitute for green onions and highly esteemed in the art of cookery.

HOW TO GROW. Leeks require 80 days from transplants and 140 days from seed. They need deep soil and plenty of water and fertilizer. Hill up with earth to produce the long, white stems. Plant them in trenches 4 to 6 inches deep and pile up soil

Some picture-gazers who saw this photo took these white radishes for turnips.

around the stems as they grow. Since it is difficult to prevent particles of soil from getting in between the leaves and causing a gritty taste when cooked, some gardeners place corrugated cardboard around the stems before earthing them up.

Squash...
Pick a good
eating size—
not bragging size

Allowing a zucchini to grow giant size robs the plant of what it takes to make more small zucchini.

Radishes in root view box filled with perfect soil, performing as they should except for 'White Icicle.'

Squashes

Except for the bush forms, these vegetables are space users. If you are a mini-gardener, use vertical space, such as a fence, a wall, or a stout trellis. Even a compost pile can serve as a place for a vine to ramble. They are sometimes grown with corn, but should be sparsely spaced.

HOW TO GROW. Direct seeding is best, but in short-season areas some gain can be made by starting in individual pots, as with melons.

Home gardeners generally find that they have underestimated the productive capability of the summer squashes. One or two zucchini plants, for example, will supply more than your family and your neighbors can use when the plant starts to bear.

Summer squash: Zucchini—the beginner gardener's delight—now comes in yellow, shades of green, gray, and black. Three of the hybrids are All-America selections: 'Aristocrat,' 'Chefini,' and 'Grazini.' Also on the zucchini recommended lists are 'Burpee Golden,' 'Burpee Hybrid,' 'Ambassador Hybrid.'

All types need space. The bush squash will spread its leaves 3-4 feet. The vining types should have from 5 to 12 feet of space, depending on the variety.

Fertilizing and watering requirements are the same as cucumbers and melons. Summer squashes, like cucumbers, should be kept picked continuously for a steady supply of young fruit. Don't worry if some of the blossoms fail to set fruit or produce small fruits that abort and rot. This is natural, and is either because there were not enough male flowers to pollinate the existing female flowers, or the plant is aborting young fruits in order to better develop the fruit already set.

HOW TO HARVEST. Summer squashes are picked when they are young and tender. The seeds should be undeveloped and the rind soft. Zucchini and crookneck types are usually taken at 1½ to 2 inches in diameter, and bush scallops at 3 to 4 inches across.

Winter squashes must be thoroughly mature to be of good quality. When picked immature they are watery and poor in flavor. Flavor is usually better after some cold weather has increased the sugar content.

For very good reasons, new varieties of squash and pumpkin are appearing each year in seed racks and catalogs. Plant breeders are adding new hybrids to the old types that are more vigorous, more disease resistant, and easier to pick.

There are more bush varieties of the running vine types for the limited space gardeners.

Winter squash: 'Gold Nugget' (85 days). Bush variety; earliest of the winter squash. 'Waltham Butternut'. (95 days). Mild flavor. 'Buttercup' (100 days). Sweet, strong flavor. 'Emerald' is a bush 'Butter-cup.' 'Table Queen' (85 days). Acorn type, early baking squash. 'Table King' is a bush type, 'Table Queen.' 'Hubbard' (110 days). Large, good keeper. 'Banana' (110 days). Long, pink, gray. Jumbo strains available.

Items that make suburban gardeners wish they had acres

In the new seed catalogs, we read items like these and think of all the seed roasting we would like to try and then we take another look for the sunny spots around the place.

Lady Godiva. "Naked" Pumpkin Seeds. 110 days. Grow your own snacks with this remarkable novelty. Developed by the U.S. Dept. of Agriculture, it is a pumpkin that produces "naked" or hull-less seeds which are delightful to eat either raw or toasted—*and they require no tedious shelling!* An attractive deep green color, they are highly nutritious and rich in proteins.

The pumpkins are yellowish, generally with green stripes or markings, and weigh about 6 lbs. The flesh is not of table quality but they are great producers of these perfectly delicious seeds.

Eat-All. New Hampshire's Sweetpotato Squash with tasty hulless seeds of high nutritional value. Marvelous flavor. Baked seeds make a wholesome confection. Green and white striped fruits on compact 5 foot vines.

Parching Corn. Here we offer properly cured White Crisp corn for home parching. To parch, corn must be brittle dry, and proceed as if popping corn with popping oil and stirring. When kernels turn autumn brown, pour out to cool. Salt and serve.

Mammoth Sunflower. 80 days. The striped seeds are plump, well-filled with meat and have a thin shell. Valuable food for poultry and song birds. Stalks are tall; excellent for backgrounds or screening purposes.

'Rhubarb chard' should be called an edible ornamental. Leaves are more tender, milder than 'Swiss chard.'

All-American-Selection of vegetables are tested in planting like these at the Calloway gardens.

Nature's forming of a head of cabbage is a performance no one should miss. Each kind, round ball, flat top, conical and crinkled savoy type has its own particular form.

Early in the life of this garden, daffodils and calendula, with nectarine blossoms overhead, mingle with chard and the first and second plantings of lettuce. A most pleasant combination for an early spring garden. Create interesting bouquet gardens with combinations of good eating and colorful blooming plants.

Plant for color and texture in your garden. Here 'Ruby Ball' cabbage and bright marigolds smile up at you. This planting grew through the warm days of July and August without bolting or splitting, The colors seem to reflect the summer sun. "Ruby" is the color of the cabbage head.

Don't let the word *vegetable* be a stumbling block

Many gardeners are seeing vegetables with new eyes—appraising them for their unique form and color *before* admitting that in common usage they are called *vegetables*.

Now it's vegetables-flowers, and flowers-vegetables and who says they don't mix?

Red cabbage, with it's surprising bluish cast, and marigolds make a striking bed, set off by a lawn beyond.

A bed of curly kale can rival the beauty of a bed of ferns.

Daffodils look elegant dancing almost everywhere—above a ground cover of parsley, or lettuce.

Gladiolus in clumps here and there look beautiful with a vine crop such as cucumbers.

Rhubarb chard, with it's translucent red stalk and crinkly leaves is a vegetable to be used almost anywhere. Try it above a river of white alyssum with white Sweet William.

Peppers, especially the small hot varieties that hold their many fruits high, should have their place in the flower border.

In a shady spot in the garden try parsley, chives and mint. Grow the mint in a sunken pot to keep the roots in bounds. And, put a little spearmint in a sunken pot right under the garden faucet.

Corn will look as tropical as ginger lilies in a large patio planter.

Okra shows its hibiscus relationship in leaf and flower in the flower border.

Try a border of beets and carrots along a walk.

Here's what the University of Nebraska has to say about squash in the garden:

"Although pumpkin and squash are primarily grown for eating, attractive 'tropical' appearing foliage, large showy yellow blossoms and interesting shapes and beautiful colors of the fruit are ornamental values giving them dual purpose usefulness."

Above left: Here's cabbage again as giant budding flowers in a flower border. Above right: The daffodils and pansies say it's spring and the leaf lettuce finds the cool weather just right for growing. Strangely, in the vegetable garden, we worry about weeds with such plants as cabbage and lettuce, but here they receive the competition of the surrounding flowers and bulbs, without apparent distress—and surely the cabbage can't distinguish between a flower and a weed. It might be that the rules of the flower border are more relaxed than those of the vegetable garden.

Above: Artichoke buds are carried above the fountain of silvery green leaves. If left to grow, buds open to form magnificent purple-blue thistlelike flowers 6 inches across. Popular in dry arrangements, the artichoke needs room to grow. Reaches 4 feet high with a spread of 6 feet or more. It's best in coastal northern California areas and climates with cool summer temperatures and mild winters. Must have winter protection in cold winter climates.

Above left: Lettuce has the distinction in form and color that is required for pattern planting. Even patterns as complex as the traditional "knot gardens" can be achieved. But it's not the most practical way to grow lettuce. Above right: This "cutting" garden, like those in old estate grounds, serves the dual function of furnishing cut flowers and fresh vegetables to the "mansion," but today's cutting garden is in no way "hidden from view."

How to avoid the strawberry stumbling block

Set the crown of the plant at ground level—neither too high or too low.

Choose varieties which are certified to be virus-free.

Choose varieties which are specifically adapted for your climate.

Special attention is usually given to strawberries in the home garden and rightfully so. Improved varieties make strawberry growing less hazardous and will provide the gardener with crop after crop of delicious strawberries.

As seen in these pictures, the strawberry can be grown successfully in a variety of situations—in containers of all kinds, in vertical gardens, in hanging baskets, with or without plastic mulch, or used as an edible ornamental serving a wide variety of landscape uses. (see pages 20, 21)

Whether growing strawberries in containers or in the garden, the soil you plant them in should be fairly rich with the addition of organic matter and well drained. If you set the plants too high in the soil the top part of the roots will dry out; if you set the crown of the plant below the surface of the soil it will rot—hence the warning, "set the crown of the plant at ground level."

Gardeners who grow strawberries in containers, in a disease-free soil mix, don't have to worry about verticillium wilt and red stele (root rot). Both are caused by soil-borne fungus. To insure success start with plants certified to be virus-free. In many states all of the varieties offered through commercial growers are certified to be virus-free. They will generally out-produce other varieties and will bear good crops for up to 3 years or more.

◁

Strawberry "tree" is half cylinder of soil mix held in place by wire mesh and sphagnum moss. See page 51. Impatiens add their color to the column.

If you have grown strawberries for several years, you know their performance is not exactly predictable. The quality of the same variety may differ from one year to the next due to differences in the weather pattern and soil conditions.

Also, if you have gardened in several locations, you learned that what is the "best" variety in one location is only fair in another area. Varieties available at local garden stores are adapted to your area. In choosing adapted varieties, you can play it safe by checking with the office of your County Agricultural Extension Agent. See pages 78, 79.

Every year new strawberry varieties appear and older varieties are dropped by commercial growers for reasons of production, performance, shipping ability and comparison taste tests. The supply at garden stores will be a mixture of the latest commercially recommended varieties and those with local appeal. Since firmness for shipping is not important in the home garden, you may not agree with the taste tests of the commercial grower.

The following are some of the recommended varieties you may run into in your area:

Varieties

'Tioga.' Midseason. California 1955. Large berries of good quality with firm flesh and tough skin. Plants produce an exceptionally heavy crop for over two months beginning in March or April. Adapted to all strawberry areas of California.

'Lassen.' Everbearing. California. Medium large berries for use fresh or for freezing. Adapted to warm winter areas. Does well in Southern California.

'Shasta.' Everbearing near coast in Northern California. Berries are very large but total crop is less than 'Tioga.'

'Sequoia.' Everbearing. Developed for coastal California. High flavor quality. Bears heavy spring crop, light in summer and a fair crop until frost. Good disease resistance.

'Hood.' Oregon introduction. Large handsome berries of medium softness and very good flavor. Top quality for canning, freezing, jams and jellies. Resistant to leaf spot, leaf scorch, red stele, and verticillium wilt.

'Ogallala.' Berries are dark red, soft and of medium size. Good flavor and good for freezing. Vigorous grower and winter hardy.

Good production in plastic pails, sunk in the ground. Ground covered with shredded fir bark.

The strawberry adapts well to container planting—pot, box, or basket—hanging or otherwise.

When crowded in containers, compensate for the lack of root space with frequent light liquid feedings.

Neat appearing strawberry planting in plastic covered beds, edged with 2x4's, with bark ground cover.

From North Willamette Oregon Experiment station, strawberries as they should produce.

One of our gardeners has experimented with planting in bricks laid in sand with one brick removed for each plant. So far this method has produced equally well to those planted under plastic and ground culture.

Wood frame of redwood designed to hold containers of recycled square plastic water jugs cut down to size.

In mild winter areas of the country no flowers are as colorful and willing to furnish late winter and early spring color as the polyanthus primroses. In cooler regions they can be started indoors for bringing outdoors as soon as temperature permits. Well adapted for display in containers.

The 'Hoop Petticoat' miniature daffodil will perform beautifully in a tea-cup size container. The little plant even loves to be handled for close-up viewing.

Here the gardener has created an "instant" garden just a week old with a brick-edged flat of Scotch moss, a brick square of Crane's bill (Erodium chamaedryoides) ground cover, blue ageratum and pots of blooming alyssum and brightly colored marigolds. Potted plants can be grown early indoors or purchased from retail growers for quick effects.

Lightweight volcanic rock is the "pot" for these Rabbit's foot ferns. They are rooted in sphagnum moss in wide shallow holes chipped out of the rock.

A brick terrace is the "planting" ground for a garden of container grown plants in all sizes and colors. Close-up of the dwarf ageratum at right.

Ways to garden when there's little or no space to garden

Finding space to garden where there's little or no space to garden, is a game that gardeners play very well. In the next 8 pages we tell and show you our experiences with the no-space garden and the good ideas of many good gardeners everywhere.

Planting plastic pails

I have struggled for a long time with poor soil, and even poorer results from my planting efforts. The thought of adding yards and yards of soil conditioners was a little frightening, not to mention expensive. I finally solved it all by the use of plastic pails. My garden plot now is row upon row of plastic pails sunk in the soil right up to ground level. This way I concentrate and control the soil in the pails only.

I used inexpensive plastic pails and drilled several holes in each for drainage. Plastic pails are now manufactured in a variety of sizes, and are available in most shopping centers. The 5 gallon size makes a good substitute for the standard 5 gallon can used in nurseries, and most vegetables and plants can be grown easily in them. I filled the pails with a light weight soil mix, sunk them in the ground, and then covered the ground around them with bark to hide the rim of the pails. Almost any annual and vegetables like squash, tomatoes, peppers and lettuce are quite happy in their plastic pails. By laying them out in rows, watering can be a simple matter done with soaker hose laid next to the pails.

A container gardener says

Until a good root system developed, I noticed that some of the soil mix I use was being flushed out the drain hole each time I watered my container plants. I now use a small piece of screening to cover the drain hole—it stops the soil from being washed out, doesn't stop drainage, and discourages slugs, sowbugs and other pests from making their home in the bottom of the containers.

Make room for water

I'll tell you one thing—watering a lot of containers can be a chore, and it's a triple chore if there's not enough space from the top of the soil to the rim of the pot, or top of the box for enough water to drain through the root ball. When soil is too close to the top you have to hit the pot or box two or three times to really water it.

Watering many containers at once

In hot, windy weather, my son and I spent almost an hour watering our 24 plant container garden. The plants were in a light soil mix and we watered slowly. We tried putting a couple of inches of sand on top of the planter mix so we could water a little faster without floating the mix away. It helped, but our best idea was the use of a length of galvanized eave trough (roof gutter) capped at both ends.

We laid it across the rims of a dozen containers in a row and used a nail to punch a hole in the bottom of the trough for each container. Now we flood the trough and it irrigates many pots at once. We also fertilize with liquid fertilizer this way. If we move a container out of the row, we plug up the unused water hole with liquid solder from a tube. When not in use the trough can be stored.

Leaky balcony gardens

We live in an upstairs apartment and have a beautiful container plant garden on our balcony, but we found out that when we watered our "garden" we were also watering the neighbors balcony below. My husband made a frame out of 2 x 2 inch redwood in the shape of the area where our plants are, and then stapled black plastic to the frame making a large plastic tray, more or less. Any drainage water is held by the plastic, and we haven't had a complaint from the neighbors since.

Don't let them sit down

We have a lot of container plants on our deck and patio, and have found that it's worth the time and effort to keep them raised up. Using saucers under pots, and small wooden blocks to keep other containers an inch or so above the ground eliminates the ring-shaped stain that occurs if the pot is not raised up. Keeping wooden containers blocked up also keeps the bottom from rotting out so fast.

The bottomless box

Over the years of container gardening I find myself with boxes and tubs once beautiful, with the bottoms rotted out, warped or otherwise not fit frontline display. Rather than breaking them up for the fireplace I recycle them. An 18 inch square bottomless box made of 2 inch cedar now holds three tomatoes trained teepee fashion. The bottomless box serves as a small raised bed in the vegetable garden. Drainage through the first 12 inches of soil is perfect, but in addition the tomatoes have unlimited root space. Theres no need to water the soil in the box as frequently as I would if the tomatoes were planted in the open soil.

Bottomless planter boxes and tubs have other advantages when used in the garden—by lining the bottom of the container with ½ inch mesh wire you can gopher-proof your favorite bulbs or any other plant.

When you go on vacation

Over the years we've tried various ways to "vacationize" our potted plants. Manufactured items for this purpose are useful, but we think we have the ideal set-up. We had a 2 x 5 foot sheet metal tray made with 3 inch sides. We made the corners of the tray water tight using a plastic sealer. We then filled the tray with 2 inches of pea gravel and filled the tray with water—just enough to cover the gravel. We set the potted plants on the gravel and used water-wicks (available at most nurseries) to transfer the water from the tray to the pots. This not only gives us automatic watering, but the fact that the plants are sitting on a moist surface gives them a better growing environment than normal.

Hanging baskets

Hanging baskets can be made from anything that will hold soil. The traditional wire frame lined with sphagnum moss has the greatest appeal to the hanging basket addict. It has the advantage in multiple plantings. Seedlings can be grown around the sides of the basket, rather than only from the tops of boxes, pots or plastic containers.

The sphagnum moss basket can be made into a suspended bouquet in a few minutes without thought about the plants trailing habits. Given wire, an inch thick lining of sphagnum, a lightweight planter mix and you are ready to arrange whatever the nursery has to offer in small sizes—dwarf marigolds, dwarf ageratum, dwarf alyssum, dianthus, impatiens, fibrous begonias.

Plant a shallow pot saucer or tray and hang to display a miniature eye-level landscape. Many interesting hangers are available or make your own.

A number of succulents are good for hanging gardens. They enjoy the warmer atmosphere of higher areas. Here is the "string-of-pearls," Senecio rowleyanus.

A tree filled with colorful summer flowers. Baskets of annuals hang from the branches of the tree which grows in the middle of a concrete patio. Different moods can be created just by changing the colors or kinds of flowers. Plant all one type for a monochromatic color scheme or create a riot of color according to your mood or the occasion.

The filtered light underneath the branches of this tree provide just the right light for summering of hanging potted house plants.

Cascading yellow chrysanthemums provide a large massive display of colorful blooms. The hanging basket container is suspended from the beams of a porch. This colorful late summer or fall "garden" provides the gardener with cut flowers for use in bouquets. Several of these baskets make a spectacular show.

Holes cut through the sphagnum moss are the planting holes for this hanging garden. What is transplanted there may be changed by the season, what's available at the nurseries and your good taste.

Rotating baskets

Turning hanging baskets to get them in the right sun exposure was a job

Fisherman's swivel for freely turning hanging basket.

for us until we tried using swivels, found in my husbands fishing tackle box. Now we can turn the baskets so that the plants grow evenly on all sides without taking the baskets down.

Don't go out on a limb

You don't have to go out on a limb to suspend a hanging basket. Tie a loop in one end of a length of nylon cord. Attach a heavy fishing sinker or other weight to the loop, and throw it over a branch; the weight will bring the loop down to you. Put the other end of line through the loop and you have a slip knot. Now pull the unlooped end to bring loop up to the branch. This makes a tight knot around the branch. Suspend the basket from the line.

Miniature roses take to the air

Rose breeder Ralph Moore reports the newest trend is to grow certain of the miniature varieties in hanging baskets. One discarded old variety, Papoose, has been brought back into cultivation because it grows so well in hanging baskets. Others recommended by Moore include Green Ice, Happy Time, Little Girl and Sugar Elf.

Suspenders

I've found a way to convert any clay or plastic pot into a hanging container, using a 1/8 or 3/16 aluminum or aluminum alloy rod. The length of the rod depends on how high or low you want to hang it, measuring from the drainage hole.

The end of the rod which goes through the drainage hole is threaded and held securely by a washer, larger than the hole and a nut—one of each on each side of the hole. Bend the top end of the rod into a hook so it can be suspended by a chain or any type of hanger. For a more permanent arrangement, cut

the aluminum rod to the desired length and thread the top of it. Attach a threaded socket to the eave or rafter where you are going to hang the basket, and attach the rod to the socket.

Since the washers block the drain hole, additional holes should be drilled using light pressure.

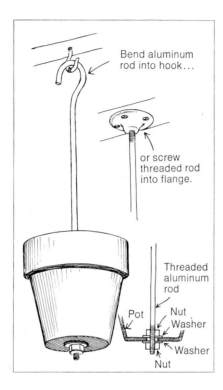

Bend aluminum rod into hook...

or screw threaded rod into flange.

Threaded aluminum rod

Pot Nut
Washer
Washer
Nut

To espalier

Originally the word *espalier* was defined as a trellis upon which a plant is trained. Now the expression *to espalier* is used loosely to mean *to train* plants to grow flat against a wall trellis, fence or free-standing panel. The training may take a formal pattern such as repeated horizontals or the plant may be allowed to develop in a natural, informal pattern.

The small space gardener may or may not be interested in espaliering. They do, however, get the idea as a space saving method. The idea that you can enjoy 3 or 4 varieties of dwarf apples on a 15 foot long trellis makes good space saving sense.

Commercial fruit growers are finding higher production of many fruits by crowding dwarf and semi-dwarf trees in hedge rows.

Remember that you can direct the pattern of growth of any plant. See pages 80 and 81.

Repeated diamond-shaped patterns are created by espalier for an interesting effect along a cement block wall.

A living checkerboard can be grown along any surface. Pyracanthia is a natural for espalier culture.

Wooden frames support a trellis of cord on which climbing plants can attach themselves, adding color to an otherwise bare wall.

These frames are now supporting a number of various climbers and doing right well. In all our future built frames we will use the hinged type—they're easy to store. The use of plastic cover to create a row greenhouse will not be tested until next winter. The amount of ventilation needed with plastic covers is always a problem to the gardener. Learn what will work for your own needs by daring to experiment.

The A-frame avoids several stumbling blocks

Training vines on a trellis of wood, wire or string or a combination of all three is one of the time honored ways of saving ground space in the garden. The home gardener and the commercial grower of pole beans has used many variations of the "pole" in giving the bean vine above-ground support.

The change that is taking place with todays gardeners is the willingness to grow anything on a trellis. Vegetables that once were considered as space wasters in the small garden are taken skyward. The small fruited watermelon, winter squash, melons and just about anything that vines is being trained vertically.

✔ *We have found the A frame type of trellis has several advantages over the vertical trellis.*

✔ *It supports itself. No heavy permanent posts are needed.*

✔ *It can be hinged to fold flat for storage.*

✔ *The frame can be converted into a tent for early spring frost protection.*

✔ *Such vegetables as pole beans and cucumbers are easy to see when the "trellis" is on a 45 to 70 degree slant. There's less chance of hiding in the leaves. And cucumbers grow straighter when hanging down.*

✔ *Large fruited vegetables that need support can be propped up on the slanting trellis with temporary ledges fitted into the trellis.*

✔ *The frame may be latticed on one side and open on the other. This variation makes for easy harvesting of vegetables that hang down.*

East-west trellis

In watching the growth of pole beans and trellised cucumbers, I found that I got a better crop if the trellis on which they were trained ran east and west. Maybe it doesn't make much difference, but by placing the trellis this way the shady north side is well suited for lettuce in the summer months.

Cucumber tower

From a small space South Carolina gardener we picked up this idea: I didn't have enough room in my garden to let cucumbers go their own way, so I made a four sided tower constructed of 2 x 2's with an exterior dimension of 2 feet by 2 feet and 6 feet high from ground level. The tower itself is constructed with cross members of 2 x 2's at the top and approximately fourteen inches from the bottom. The tower is then driven into the ground approximately 12 inches. I covered the tower with 4 inch square sweet pea netting which affords easy access to cucumbers which form inside the tower. I figure that in a 4 foot square area, I get 48 square feet of growing area for the plants.

These towers could be placed in a row and spaced 3 feet apart which would allow anyone with a limited space to grow a tremendous number of vine crops. The foliage is heavier, greener, healthier and the blossom set is far superior to that of cucumbers growing on the ground.

Supporting heavy fruits

Our panel of gardeners report the building of special shelves on fences or vertical trellises to support heavy fruits such as melons and squash. Some support the fruit in slings made of old nylon stockings.

Various forms of vertical growing as developed in our gardens

More than 10 years ago we began our search for more *growing* space in every square foot of ground space. Our starting point was a "Petunia Tree" we saw in Salt Lake City. All of our initial trials (see illustrations) were with vertical gardens built in much the same manner as a wire hanging basket. The building materials were wire mesh, sphagnum moss, and light weight planter mix. Growth of plants in these "trees" was better than expected. We grew all kinds of

lettuce, tomatoes and cucumbers as "salad trees"; marigolds, alyssum, iberis, campanula and violas, gave the trees seasonal color.

In the early days we over-scaled the units; there was no need for the amount of planter mix we used. The column we found most useful was the half circle of wire nailed or stapled to a 1 by 12-inch redwood board. Excellent growth of strawberries, vegetables and flowers occurred in half-circles of no more than 6 inches in diameter. In effect, we took a 5 foot-long row of plants in a 12-inch mounded raised bed and stood it on end.

The size of the wire mesh was important. All were planted with transplants. Although the root ball can be squeezed through a very small opening, we soon used only hog wire or welded wire with 2-inch mesh.

In the evolution of column vertical gardens we changed from sphagnum moss to black plastic film to hold the soil mix. And we became choosey about the soil mix. We used only the light weight mixes packaged to the Cornell or University of California formula. See page 11.

In appearance, the black film is not as gardenesque as sphagnum moss but the plants soon cover the plastic and we seem to get earlier growth as compared to the sphagnum vertical garden.

Petunia tree history

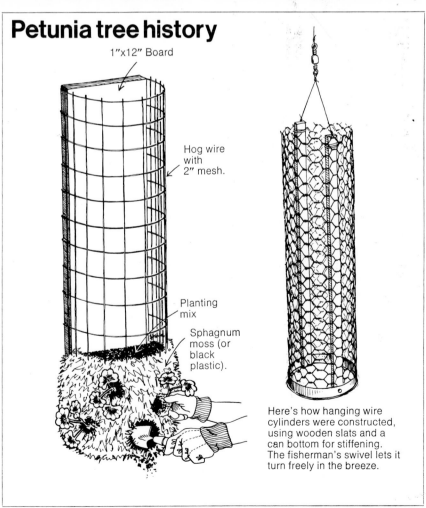

1"x12" Board

Hog wire with 2" mesh.

Planting mix

Sphagnum moss (or black plastic).

Here's how hanging wire cylinders were constructed, using wooden slats and a can bottom for stiffening. The fisherman's swivel lets it turn freely in the breeze.

The vertical garden gets wheels

In the last 2 years we have experimented with a vertical roll-a-round box as shown in these photographs. In early spring the box was planted with lettuce—leaf lettuce, butterhead, and romaine. In the summer, the box, in a part-shade position, was planted with fibrous begonias, impatiens and coleus.

The box could be any height. We made it 50 inches high. Cross pieces are 1 by 2 inches, with openings 8 inches square.

In some of the boxes we have built, we made no provision for special watering. With these there was a tendency to overwater the top part to be sure that all the soil was moist. At present we are watering through pipes placed the full depth of the box. The pipes are made of regular 1¼ inch plastic pipe, with ¼ inch holes drilled throughout the pipe.

Pipes are placed 6 inches apart in the box, as it is being filled with the soil mix.

Don't underestimate the weight of such boxes. The soil mix is light weight, but when water is added (weighing 8.3 pounds per gallon), you have a real weight problem.

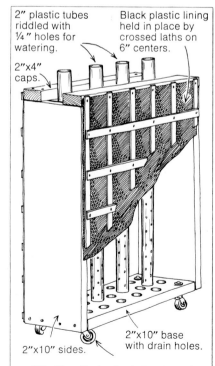

2" plastic tubes riddled with ¼" holes for watering.

Black plastic lining held in place by crossed laths on 6" centers.

2"x4" caps.

2"x10" sides.

2"x10" base with drain holes.

Fill with soil mix. Cut holes through plastic to insert small plants.

The most useful ingredient— sphagnum moss

The principle of the growing method in all forms of vertical gardening— trellis, walls, fence panels and wire hanging baskets is the same. Plant roots are in a soil mix or sphagnum moss held in place by wire or wire mesh. The size of the mesh openings should be big enough to allow for setting in transplants.

In narrow spaces, such as the fence panels at right, sphagnum moss alone is the best rooting medium. (If sphagnum moss wasn't so hard to come by we would use it as a "soil" in many verticals.)

Don't confuse sphagnum moss with sphagnum peat moss, which is a partially decayed or inert product. The sphagnum moss we are talking about *grows* in bogs and it is not decomposed. In its natural state the moss-like fibers will span openings in wire and wire mesh. This is the unmilled sphagnum moss. The milled or ground-up sphagnum has long been the favored seed starting medium for difficult-to-germinate seeds. It is sterile, eliminates "damping off," gives perfect aeration with excellent water holding ability.

Unmilled sphagnum as the "soil" for narrow panels is generally fed and watered in the same operation with a very diluted solution of liquid fertilizer.

To build a vertical garden just build a fence as shown in the drawing using 4"x4" posts and a grid of 2"x4"s. Cover the back with regular fencing material (grape stakes, 1"x6" boards, etc.), fill in the areas you wish to plant with sphagnum moss and cover it with wire mesh. Welded wire fencing with 2"x2½" mesh is ideal. Smaller mesh makes it difficult to plant through.

Before planting.

Before planting wet the moss thoroughly with a starting solution. Set transplants through the mesh—peat pots make it much easier to keep the root ball intact. Keep the moss moist always; feed frequently with a good liquid plant food solution.

Here are two checkerboard patterns created in vertical gardens built onto fences. The diagram at left shows how to construct and plant the growing pockets which are stuffed with sphagnum. Roots of the plants are inserted into the moist moss. Trailing plants or annuals adapt best to this method. Try growing a wall of herbs, alone or mixed with summer flowers.

Colorful primroses grow at eye level on a back yard fence. Roots are anchored in sphagnum stuffed into a wire frame.

An old bicycle wheel nailed to a fence provides an unusual support for growing beans, a living sculpture.

One planting of flowering cabbage

produces as many forms and colors as

there are plants. They need near freezing

weather to show color. Plan plantings for

late fall-winter maturity.

With a free hand and a light heart

That seems to be one of the best ways to enjoy your garden.

Nature has some unexpected delights in for the accepting gardener.

No plant ever asked a gardener for his credentials in gardening.

Some of the most meaningful words for our time were written by L. H. Bailey in 1898. They are as true now as they were then:

"Every family can have a garden. If there is not a foot of land, there are porches or windows. Wherever there is sunlight, plants may be made to grow; and one plant in a tin can may be a more helpful and inspiring garden to some mind than a whole acre of lawn and flowers may be to another."

"The satisfaction of a garden does not depend upon the area, nor, happily, upon the cost or rarity of the plants. It depends upon the temper of the person. One must first seek to love plants and nature, and then to cultivate that happy peace of mind which is satisfied with little. He will be happier if he has no rigid and arbitrary ideals for gardens are coquettish, particularly with the novice. If the plants which thrive chance not to be the ones he planted, they are plants nevertheless, and nature is satisfied with them."

"We are apt to covet the things which we cannot have; but we are happier when we love the things which grow because they must."

"The man who worries morning and night about the dandelions in the lawn will find great relief in loving the dandelions. Each blossom is worth more than a gold coin, as it shimmers in the exuberant sunlight of the growing spring, and attracts the bees to its bosom. Little children love the dandelions: why may not we? Love the things nearest at hand; and love intensely."

Into our gardens the wind, or imported soil can bring with it new plants. In a shady area, a fern may appear quite unexpectedly. Since it chose to make its home in your garden, it must like it there. It may grow better than the plants you have chosen for the spot.

Geraniums often seem to go their own way. The one you planted and nourished may grow leggy and unhealthy looking. And lo and behold, one day, there is a geranium poking its flowering head out of the hedge. It's always a marvel to see a geranium, full of blossoms, and sculptured by the weather next to a rarely used cottage.

As Bailey says, "If a person wants to show his skill, he may choose the balky plant; but if he wants fun and comfort in gardening, he had better choose the willing one."

So, plant what grows best for you, and accept what nature adds to your garden. Real satisfaction lies in success for most gardeners.

Left alone, plants will do their own thing. Just because the plant book may say a pittosporum is a shrub doesn't mean that the plant knows that is what it is supposed to be. You may look around some years later and find it fifteen feet tall with a trunk six inches around. Whether or not it achieves those proportions depends upon your discrete pruning.

Plants will respond in all sorts of ways to the right touch. A loving gardener can direct the growth of a plant north, south, east and west with the greatest of ease. It takes the feel of the plant and dedicated "pinching-off."

There are so many things that can be done with form. Take for instance the different forms of trellises and structures and a plant such as a wisteria.

Vines can be woven together to form green and flowering garlands. Often the vine itself will decide to climb a telephone line. The gardener can be a sculptor. If his interest wanes, the plant won't mind, it will take its own form and create a new pattern.

The choice and placement of plants depends upon the gardener. The success of the planting depends upon the gardener's touch and the environment. A mixed grouping may be just right along a fence; plants with striking form such as bamboo, or podocarpus, may create a special atmosphere when silhouetted against translucent glass. The light hand plays an important part in these plantings.

An old brick wall was doubled in width with brick laid in sand to become a changeable gardener's playground. The space of one brick or more became the potential planting space, creating infinite possibilities for plant arrangement. Dwarf plants, moss, rock plants were favored plant materials to fit into the multiple openings. But the planting pattern today may not be the pattern tomorrow. Arrangement is limited to imagination.

Dwarf ferns and spike moss (Selaginella) look as if they grew naturally out of this lava rock. Planting spaces are chiseled out and filled with soil mix and sphagnum moss; light frequent watering is a must.

Because of its good taste, one of our gardeners is trying to bring the wild Miner's lettuce into his garden.

Create ivy hoops or clematis umbrellas. Design any kind of wire form and you'll find a vine that is willing to grow on it.

Column of spring bloom was grown horizontally on wire covered board and up-ended for special display. See page 51 for instructions.

Baskets as containers give plants the look of a bouquet not possible with clay or plastic pots.

Clay turtle, native to Mexico, serves as container and here carries the colorful foliaged dwarf nandina.

With all the patterned colors of coleus this old owl could have an infinite change of head-dress.

Wide basket holds seedlings of red lettuce, and endive, young radishes all headed for the salad bowl.

Sewer pipes and tile flues come in all shapes and sizes. Plant them either anchored in the ground or as a pot, shown here resting on a cement square for drainage. Effects are unlimited.

This stylized tile scarecrow grows a pepper plant for a head, and has extended arms of tile and marigolds with hands of alyssum. He keeps watch over this container garden planted in unusual tile and terracota shapes. Check your building supply for unusual forms in which to plant. Add a touch of humor to your garden and express a relaxed feeling about the growing scene.

If you plan to be away from your garden for periods of time which make regular watering and care impractical, fill your garden with plants that are native to the area. There are probably already some growing in your garden. Each locale has its own varieties which are resistant to usual changes in the weather. And, you can add a few others of which you are fond that you suspect will be able to adapt to your garden outline; if they don't work out, experiment some more.

Succulents have a natural affinity for rocks, too. They can tuck themselves into the smallest of spaces in a rock or in the chink of a wall. One of the most pleasing arrangements of succulents we've seen is a beach front planting in a large piece of drift wood—even the salt doesn't seem to bother them.

Unusual containers

Take a look around for unusual containers that will give unique form to your garden. Sewer pipes and tile flues come in all shapes and sizes. They can be set into the ground, or sit on top, depending upon what you plant inside. They give you the chance to make your own soil mix to suit the plants you choose.

If you are fortunate enough to own a piece of sculpture that will survive outdoors, put it out! Surround it with a setting of flowers and green leaves. It can be the accent for a special section of your garden.

As we see this gardener, the plants smile upon her. A vine will suggest a special way to climb or angle across a wall. Plants will creep out of crevices to spread their leaves over harsh pavement. There is the one rock, one juniper restful place. Spearmint in a pot will curve over a wire hoop. There is no strain for special effects. Rosemary will drape over a wall; periwinkle will drop strands from a second story planter box. Who knows what will grow from the old flower seeds at the bottom of last year's seed box? What seeds did the birds bring in? What did the squirrel bury and forget?

Let there be soil ready for growing, be a little careless in your gardening; live a little, laugh a little with a plant.

A successful garden reflects the person who created it. Whether the garden is in the window sill, or surrounds the house, it is the light hand, not the heavy heart that must prevail if plants are to grow with ease and give joy to the planter.

Collectors who can't throw away anything from the mountains or the seashore have the material for impromptu "garden shows" especially if much of the garden is mobile or container grown. Here the imaginative gardener has combined collected stones, cement forms and weathered boards as the setting for pots of chrysanthemums and succulents. Consider the possibilities.

Rocks and succulents are natural companions. Collect large stones or buy lava rock and hollow out, place growing media in hole and plant succulent. The rocks give good, quick drainage. Varying sizes of pot saucers, shown in lower right, can be used for a stepped up series of circular plantings. You can mix succulent species or devote each of the tiers to a different group.

There are many challenges and pitfalls when you ride a plant hobby

When you fall in love with a plant—one with many possibilities of exploration—you may find yourself with a number of uncharted factors. What will the color be? How tall will it get? How hardy is it? That's when you need the help of friends, near and far, who are facing similar challenges.

One good reason for the formation of the many plant societies of America is the opportunity to share experiences; learning from others who have walked the path of discovery. Sharing experiences through plant societies comes with leaflets, bulletins, books, meetings and other activities and publications.

So, if any plant is special to you—why not join the plant society of its name. Here are a few of their addresses:

American Begonia Society

Secretary: Ms. Betty Burrel,
14050 Ramona Drive,
Whittier, CA 90605.
Annual dues: $4.00.
Monthly publication: "The Begonian."

American Bonsai Society

Secretary, Herbert R. Brawner,
229 North Shore Drive,
Lake Waukomis, Parkville, MO 64151.
Annual dues: $10.00.
Quarterly publication,
"The Bonsai Journal."

American Boxwood Society

Boyce, VA 22620. Annual dues: $5.00.
Quarterly publication: "The Boxwood Bulletin."

American Daffodil Society

89 Chicherster Rd., New Canaan, CT 06840. Annual dues: $5. Quarterly publication: "Daffodil Journal." Available to non-members: "The Daffodil Handbook," 240 pages, illus., $3.40 ppd.

American Dahlia Society

Treasurer: Lewis M. Culp,
163 Grant St., Dover, NJ 07801.
Annual dues: $6.00.
Quarterly Bulletin and Annual Classification Book.

American Fern Society

Dept. of Botany, Univ. of Rhode Island, Kingston, RI 02881.
Annual dues: $5.00.
Quarterly publication: "American Fern Journal;" also quarterly Newsletter.

American Fuchsia Society

Secretary: Fred J. Clark,
1600 Prospect St., Belmont, CA 94002.
Annual dues: $4.00.
Monthly publication: "Bulletin of the American Fuchsia Society."

American Gesneriad Society

Secretary: Edmund O. Sherer,
11983 Darlington Avenue,
Los Angeles, CA 90049.
Annual dues: $5.25.
Bi-monthly magazine.

American Gloxinia & Gesneriad Society

Secretary: Mrs. J. W. Rose,
Box 174, New Milford, CT 06776.
Annual dues: $5.00.
Bi-monthly publication:
"The Gloxinian."

American Gourd Society

Secretary: John Stevens,
Box 274, Mount Gilead, OH 43338.
Annual dues: $2.50.
Publication three times yearly:
"The Gourd."

American Hemerocallis Society

Secretary: Mrs. Arthur W. Parry,
Signal Mountain, TN 37377.
Annual dues: $5.00.
Quarterly publication:
"The Hemerocallis Journal."

American Hibiscus Society

Secretary: James E. Monroe,
Box 98, Eagle Lake, FL 33839.
Annual dues: $5.00.
Quarterly publication:
"The Seed Pod."

American Hosta Society

Secretary: Mrs. Nancy Minks,
114 The Fairway,
Albert Lea, MN 56007.
Annual dues: $3.00.
Annual Bulletin plus newsletters.

American Iris Society

Secretary: Clifford W. Benson, Missouri Botanical Garden, 2315 Tower Grove Ave., St. Louis, MO 63110.
Annual dues: $7.50. Quarterly publication: "AIS Bulletin."

American Magnolia Society

Secretary: Philip J. Savage, 2150 Woodward Ave., Bloomfield Hills, MI 48013. Annual dues: $5.00. Illustrated newsletters.

American Orchid Society

Botanical Museum of Harvard Univ., Cambridge, MA 02138. Annual dues: $12.50. Monthly publication: "American Orchid Society Bulletin."

American Penstemon Society

Secretary: Mrs. F. J. Schmeeckle, R. 2, Box 61, Cozad, NB 69130.
Annual dues: $3.00. Annual Bulletin.

American Peony Society

Secretary: Greta M. Kessenrich, 250 Interlachen Rd., Hopkins, MN 55343. Annual dues: $7.50.
Quarterly Bulletin.

American Plant Life Society and The American Amaryllis Society Group

Secretary: Dr. Thomas W. Whitaker, Box 150, La Jolla, CA 92038.
Annual dues: $5.00.
Annual combined publication: "Plant Life; Amaryllis Yearbook."

American Rock Garden Society

Secretary: Milton S. Mulloy, 99 Pierpont Rd., Waterbury, CT 06705.
Annual dues: $5.00. Quarterly Bulletin.

American Rose Society

4048 Poselea Pl., Columbus, OH 43214. Annual dues: $10.50. Monthly publication: "American Rose;" "American Rose Annual."

Bromeliad Society

Membership Secretary,
Box 3279, Santa Monica, CA 90403.
Annual dues: $7.50.
Bi-monthly publication: "Journal."

Herb Society of America

300 Massachusetts Ave., Boston, MA 02115. Annual dues: $12.50.
Annual publication: "The Herbalist."

International Geranium Society

Secretary: C. W. Rager, 2547 Blvd. Del Campo, San Luis Obispo, CA 93401, Annual dues: $4.00. Publication: "Geraniums Around the World."

National Oleander Society

President: Mrs. Cortus T. Koehler, 5127 Ave. O-½, Galveston, TX 77550.
Annual dues: $5.00.

Roses... Easy and beautiful

Roses grow and flourish in every climate of the United States and Canada. They take, in stride, humid days and nights, the dry desert's highest temperatures and strongest winds, and the cool fog of the seashore. Roses have a strong will to grow and a wonderful responsiveness to the gardener's attention.

Every year the American Rose Society (see page 59 for address) publishes a little "Handbook for Selecting Roses." One of the features is a tabulation of "High Rated Roses By Color." Pictured here are some of the high achievers from over the years. (From top left to right) Tropicana, Pascali, Tiffany and two favorites, Queen Elizabeth and Peace.

HOW MUCH WATER? If you want to cripple a rose, let it get under stress from lack of water. If soil drainage is adequate, you can't give a rose too much water. At the same time the old warning "roses can't stand wet feet" still holds. When water moves through the soil, air in the soil is not driven out—and there's no trouble. However, when water fills the soil and doesn't drain away, it drives out soil air and roots drown—and that means trouble.

In areas where soil may be flooded for any period of time, or where the water table is high, better grow your roses in raised beds.

Prune as they grow—a rose bush responds to constant grooming—cutting out weak and spindly shoots, removing old flowers as soon as they have passed their peak, cutting out suckers (shoots that originate from below the graft union).

Flowers of the hybrid teas are produced in waves. Allowing the plant to set seeds, increases the interval between waves of bloom. When removing fading flowers don't just snip off the flower; cut back to a 5-leaflet leaf. Exceptions to such cut backs are: during the first growing season of a newly planted rose just snip the flowers (a young plant needs all the leaves it can produce); in cold winter areas, allow the seed pods (hips) to form on the final wave of bloom. Formation of hips slows down growth and hardens the plant for the winter ordeal.

MULCHING—you can grow good roses without mulching—but you can grow even better roses, with less time and trouble, if you use a mulch. Keep soil temperatures down in hot summer months with a 2 inch layer of organic mulch such as ground bark, coarse bark chunks, or peat moss, or a locally available mulch. Mulching material breaks down quickly, especially during hot months—so renew mulches yearly.

Special effect with roses such as these trained on an archway.

Roses come in all shapes and sizes. With all the different classifications, there is surely a rose to fit most any landscape need.

Some of the classifications include: Climber, Climbing Hybrid Tea, Climbing Miniature, Climbing Floribunda, Floribunda, Grandiflora, and Hybrid Musk.

The challenge of camellia collecting

What makes camellia growing so special? There are more than 3000 named kinds of camellias varying in form, size, color, and climate adaptation. With this diversity, many a gardener has found the camellia adventure to be one part growing and nine parts collecting the jewels of the plant world.

The camellia adventure is one you can jump into. No previous gardening experience is necessary. Just join your nearest camellia society and you are on your way. You'll jump from novice to expert by the third meeting. (see page 90 for address of the American Camellia Society)

When to plant: Shop your local nurseries from October to March when camellias are in bloom. Mid-season varieties are the best bets where fall temperatures are high and hot weather may come in April.

How to plant: the soil for camellias should drain well yet retain moisture. To get this combination, spread peat moss or other organic matter 3 inches deep over the planting bed and mix thoroughly with the top 12 inches of soil. Water thoroughly to settle soil mix. Set the root ball slightly above the surface of the soil.

To protect surface roots, add a 2-inch mulch of pine, straw, bark, etc.

Plant above ground in raised beds if soil is heavy clay or drainage is restricted by high water table or hardpan.

Growing in pots and tubs: there are advantages to container growing — with a prepared soil mix you can grow camellias regardless of native soil, and it's hard to find a better patio plant.

Pruning and disbudding: One way to maintain the shape of the plant is to take two or three leaves with the bloom when cutting flowers. You can save one bud out of a cluster without damaging the one you want by piercing a small hole from the tip of the bud downward. Air enters the bud and it will dry and fall naturally.

Here are some of the best reasons for joining the Camellia Society—and these are just hints at the hundreds of possible variations on the camellia theme. From top left reading down you see, 'Mark Alan,' 'Sawadas Dream,' 'Betty Sheffield Supreme,' 'Crimson Robe,' 'Kick Off,' 'Sam Barranco Pink,' 'Valentines Day,' 'Tinsie,' 'Pink Poppy,' 'First Prom,' 'Magnoliaeflora.'

Crocus defy the weather and though temporary with their bloom seem to put an end to winter even as it lingers on. The flowers in many shades of yellow, lavender and white seem to carpet the earth for the entrance of spring.

Stumbling blocks with bulbs are few and far between

Plant a daffodil bulb in October or November and come spring, right on schedule, there's a daffodil dancing in the garden. It's difficult to think of ways you can stop the daffodil from performing in the very same fashion as pictured in the catalogs — unless someone switched the label.

Bulbs reward the gardener when planted generously against flowering shrubs such as azaleas. Dozens of daffodil varieties can be naturalized.

Species tulips such as 'Bright Gem' and 'Dasystemon' are most effective in containers and in drifts in rock gardens or use in clumps here and there.

This promise-made, promise-kept picture of bulb growing needs a few ''if's'' — so heed the following:

It's a good idea to know how to pick a sound bulb when choosing them at the garden store. Choose them in the same manner you would an onion in the grocery store — bulbs should be firm when pressed and have a tight ''jacket'' covering them.

Buy bulbs as early as you can from garden centers — they usually arrive in early September — to be sure of getting the varieties you want. Store the bulbs in a cold area until you are ready to plant them.

Depth-to-plant charts are shown wherever bulbs are sold and appear in all bulb catalogs. We follow the old rule of thumb — ''plant bulbs 2 to 3 times their own depth'' — except when planting them in heavy, poorly-drained soil, then plant them a little shallower so there's less chance of rotting.

The first year the number and size of the flowers are set by the size of the bulb — all the more reason to buy first quality, large bulbs in the first place — and you cannot change them by fertilizing. However, you can influence the leaf growth for next year's bulb growth. Feed bulbs every 2 weeks after the first true leaves appear with a liquid fertilizer at ½ the recommended rate. Keep the leaves growing as long as you can. The more leaf growth, the more food is stored in the bulb for next season's flowers.

After the bulbs bloom, continue to water them. Tuck drying leaves under annuals, or tie and braid them together as they turn yellow. Do not remove the leaves until they have withered to a point that you can pull them up with a very slight effort.

Tulips are especially effective when massed at the lawn's edge or given space with flowering trees. These bulbs are many gardeners' favorites because of the great variety of form and color available.

Beautiful lily-shaped tulips are elegant in naturalized plantings scattered throughout the garden. Plant one kind in mass or mix many hues and forms.

Bulbs in containers

As the photographs on these pages demonstrate, bulbs enjoy life in containers. And (if you are concentrating your gardening) in the warm winter areas it's a good idea to limit the growing of hardy bulbs — tulips, hyacinth, and crocus — to pots and boxes. These hardy bulbs require 6 weeks or more of winter chilling at about 40 degrees in order to trigger the normal development of leaf, stem and flower.

If you wish to enjoy their classic forms you can give them the necessary chilling by placing them in the refrigerator (not the freezer) for 6 weeks and then planting out in November or December.

Forcing bulbs for winter color

If you want to concentrate your garden and enjoy spring-flowering bulbs even in the greyest of winter months, consider the florist' method of *forcing* bulbs. The steps involved are quite simple:

Step one   Choose a container—clay pot, ceramic bowl or what-have-you—that is at least twice as high as the bulb. (This will allow for adequate root development.) The container must have a drainage hole at the bottom. Fill with a light planter mix. Plant the bulbs shoulder to shoulder for full effect. The tips of the bulbs should protrude above the soil surface. Water thoroughly by setting container in pail of water and letting it soak until the surface of the soil feels moist.

Step two   Place containers where they can get 12 to 14 weeks of "cold" treatment—temperatures between 40-50°. Any spot that's cold and dark is satisfactory. An unheated cellar or vegetable storage unit is ideal. A covered cold frame outdoors will do the job. Outdoors pots should be covered with peat moss or sawdust. The purpose of the storage period is to give the bulbs the chilling they require and to develop a strong root system. Roots require moisture for growth. Soil should be moist when containers go into storage and kept moist throughout the storage treatment.

Step three   When the sprouts of the bulbs are 2 to 5 inches high and the roots can be seen at the drainage hole, place the container in a cool 60° room. After a week or two they are ready to take normal room temperatures.

Daffodils come out of their fall and winter root-growth period to be moved to a cool bright place indoors for early forced bloom. Indoors or out, daffodils herald the coming of spring and brighten the gardener's eye. Many species and varieties of daffodils are available in subtle to brilliant shades.

Upper left: The autumn-flowering Colchium *will grow without water or soil. Plant in soil after the flowering and green foliage will develop. Upper right: Ornithogalum arabicum, the "Arab's Eye." Lower left: Iris reticulata. Lower right: Crocus chysantus 'Snowbunting' for early spring.*

Of something old— something new

Gardeners have a way of never forgetting the past—or at least the best of past. By their swings in mood, they build a strong continuity in the history of gardening.

About the time the plant breeder reaches new plateaus in giving us "bigger and better, fully double" varieties, gardeners rediscover the simple, old-styled single variety.

This point was illustrated to us the other day when a gardener friend was surprised to find that you could still buy hollyhock seed; she hadn't seen a plant, or seeds for hollyhocks, in a long time. When we showed her a picture of the new varieties, double, ruffled and improved, she said, "Oh, that doesn't look like the hollyhock that I remember."

A check with the seed catalogs reveals many *discoveries* of old forms scattered among the new.

Side by side in the *Burpee Seed* catalog we found the new dwarf, double-flowering nasturtiums, as well as the old variety of single-flowering nasturtiums which they describe as, "Old-fashioned charm makes single-flowered nasturtiums in great demand for garden and cutting."

In the *Nichols Garden Nursery* catalog from Oregon, we found this link with the past: "Black Aztec Sweet Corn. This corn is unadulterated by any outside strain, and is identical to that which Aztec farmers grew 2,000 years ago. It has the same sweetness and flavor it had then. Vigorous grower and large producer of average size ears. Kernels are white in young milk stage, then turn jet black when kernels are dried. The ground corn makes a wonderful corn meal to use for baking and cooking."

The recent popularity of hanging baskets has caused many gardeners to see some plants in a new light. One of the oldest varieties of zinnias, 'Zinnia linearis' has been resurrected because of its impressive performance in hanging baskets. It grows to a height of 8-inches and will trail. When in full bloom it is covered with small, golden orange flowers, each petal with a lemon stripe.

And what is it about a bushy red geranium in a moss-covered clay pot that seems to say "gardening"? Geraniums have been popular in homes and gardens since before the American Revolution. They have gone through many changes in breeding; improving the plant and flower greatly, but the geranium still retains its old-fashioned quality. Versatility and a failure proof reputation have always been their big appeal.

All geraniums grow well in containers and hanging baskets, and most are true indoor-outdoor plants. If growing indoors, give geraniums a sunny warm spot. For best blooming results keep the plant somewhat potbound.

Another endearing quality is that geraniums start easily from cuttings. If your neighbor has a favorite plant you've been eyeing, snip off one of the stems about 4 to 6 inches long and take the lower leaves off. It will root quickly if poked into a light soil and kept evenly moist.

In recent years geranium breeders have finally perfected strains which grow "true" from seed. Geraniums are as easy to grow from seed as they are from cuttings. The added advantage of starting geraniums from seed is their use as an annual in the spring and summer garden. Most varieties require about 120 days from seed to first bloom, so start seed indoors in February for mid-July bloom. These geraniums will bloom freely until frost at which time they can be potted up and brought indoors for winter color.

1. Lass O'Gorrie	17. Skies of Italy
2. Contrast	18. Mrs. Strong (Double
3. Blazonry	Mrs. Pollock)
4. Distinction	19. Mrs. Henry Cox
5. Display	20. Jubilee (true)
6. Mrs. Burdett Coutts	21. Mrs. Pollock
7. Greetings	22. Mrs. Parker
8. Crystal Palace Gem	23. Attraction
9. Dwarf Gold Leaf	24. Variegated Kleiner
10. Mrs. J. C. Mappin	Liebling (dwarf type)
11. Medallion	25. Variegated Prince
12. Prince Bismarck	Rupert
13. Bronze Beauty	(scented leaf)
14. Marshall MacMahon	26. Flower of Spring
(true)	27. L'Elegante (Mme.
15. Sophia Dumaresque	Margot) (Ivy type)
16. Happy Thought	

Geraniums enjoy a failure-proof reputation.

Potted geraniums are ideal for sunny windows, patios, or additions to small gardens. Pinch to keep the plant compact.

These leaves from 27 different fancy-leafed geraniums grown for their foliage represent just a sampling of the great variety of geraniums. Others are grown primarily for flower color or spicy fragrances.

Mother Nature never made a "house plant"

The more the home gardener realizes and understands that fact, the sooner he is freed from many of the restrictions that have been built up by innumerable house plant publications over the years.

Houses are built to give their owners a more comfortable climate. More often than not the indoor climate is characterized by low humidity and a fairly even 72° temperature—not exactly the ideal conditions for growing plants.

On the other hand, if you wanted to grow perfect house plants you could convert your living room into a greenhouse—the plants would thrive and the people would suffer. In between these two extremes a climate can be created where people and plants can live comfortably under the same roof—all it takes is an understanding of an indoor climate and the requirements of a plant growing indoors.

The temperature and humidity inside most houses are more closely allied to that of the desert than of the tropics, which most "house plants" call home. There are a number of ways you can boost the humidity for indoor plants short of converting your living room into a greenhouse.

Group plants together in a large planter and place moist sphagnum moss around them, or set individual pots on the surface of pebbles in a shallow plastic or metal tray. Keep water in the tray so bases of the pots never touch the water. Try small glasses of water set among the plants.

Spraying leaves often with tepid water helps increase humidity as well as keeping the foliage clean and healthy. If plants are in an area where floors, walls or furniture can be harmed from the water mist, use a large piece of cardboard or plastic as a protection.

Top photo: A) Monstera deliciosa (Philodendron pertusum); *B)* Ficus lyatra *or* F. pandurata; *C)* Philodendron laciniatum; *D)* Asplenium nidus; *E)* Begonia rex; *F)* Hedera helix; *G)* Pilea cadierei; *H)* Chamadorea elegans.
Bottom photo: A) Brassaia *(Schefflera);* *B)* Dieffenbachia picta 'Superba'; *C)* Dracaena deremensis; *D)* Cycas revoluta; *E)* Columnea 'Stavanger'; *F)* Guzmania berteroniana 'rubra'; *and* *G)* Anthurium crystallinum.

Duplicate a tropical environment and enjoy year-round colorful orchid blooms like in this Hawaiian home.

Beautiful container grown plants can be placed wherever desired for interior accents when in their prime.

House plants can be grouped together not only to create a beautiful interior area, but a more humid atmosphere to mutually benefit each other and their owners.

Enclosed gardens such as terrariums assure moist atmosphere. A large growing area can be covered in clear polyethylene to create the same effect, similar to an instant greenhouse.

Kitchens and bathrooms are natural places for higher humidity because of running water and escaping steam.

A relatively inexpensive humidifier can be added to your central heating system, creating a more desirable climate for both the plants and people. Portable room vaporizers are beneficial to plant collections.

Once you've increased the humidity in the air surrounding your plants, you've won a major portion of the battle—the balance is made up of soil, water and sunlight.

SOIL—experimenting with the proper proportions of sand, leaf mold, vermiculite and other ingredients, to come up with your own soil mix is fine if you've got the time and you don't mind a few failures along the way. The sure-fire method is to use a pre-packaged sterilized soil mix. It's clean, easy to use and not expensive. The universities have done the experimentation for you and have come up with a nearly perfect growing medium for all indoor plants. More information on the various soil mixes available appears on page 11.

WATER—while each house plant has its own requirements for water, a few basics apply to the subject.

1.) When you water, water thoroughly, so water drains out of bottom of the pot within a few minutes after watering. If the water doesn't drain out you haven't watered enough.

2.) One rule of thumb for watering is to use your finger—press your finger into the soil an inch or so; if you can feel moisture the plant is o.k. for another couple of days. Or use your eyes—if a plants leaves are drooping, water immediately and thoroughly; the plant will respond quickly and forgive you for your neglect.

3.) Don't overwater—roots need air as well as water. If you overwater, the water takes the place of the air in the soil and the plant "drowns." If you use your finger you won't have a problem of overwatering, especially if you use a prepared soil mix; these are formulated to drain quickly and retain a healthy amount of water for the roots.

SUNLIGHT—when a nurseryman tells you that the house plant you've just bought needs "a lot of light," he doesn't mean direct sunlight. There are very few houseplants that can stand direct sunlight, especially when it is intensified through a window. Like watering, different plants have different light requirements. The plants that are easiest to grow are the ones that are the most tolerant of varying light conditions (see the Indestructible list).

Plants with more specific light requirements will tell you when they are unhappy with their location. An asparagus fern that sends out a seven-foot runner or a coleus that gets "leggy" is searching for more light. When a plant's leaves wither or turn brown and crisp, it usually means it's getting too much light. Remember—not enough light will elongate, or make a plant "leggy"—too much light will stunt a plant's growth and usually cause burning of the leaves.

FERTILIZING—a house plant cannot go very far to get the food it needs; it's up to you to provide the plant with a well-balanced diet. There are a number of good, all-purpose liquid fertilizers available at nurseries and other stores. Most plants will benefit from fertilizer that is applied half-strength twice a month, rather than full strength once a month. And remember to water your plants before you fertilize them; fertilizer applied to dry soil is sometimes a shock to the plant.

Once you understand the basics of indoor gardening, walk around the house to find different climates in different rooms. The bathroom and kitchen usually have higher humidity levels than the rest of the house. A screened-in porch will have a climate similar to that of outdoors, while a bedroom may stay dark and cool most of the time.

You can try different plants in different rooms; the plant will respond to its new location in a week or so, letting you know whether or not it's happy. If your piggyback plant is happiest sitting on top of your refrigerator, even though you can't understand why—leave it there.

You soon begin to understand all plants—respecting their personalities and requirements, and the plant responds back by flourishing. It is a congenial relationship, and plants that flourish soon become a member of the family.

Experimental, adventurous gardeners sometimes violate iron-clad rules and restrictions with success. We know of some who have moved bamboo, Podocarpus, oleander, dwarf citrus trees, and Japanese maples indoors and grown them there for many years. It's a case of knowing the particular climate of a room and responding to the requirements of particular plants.

We have no intention of throwing a stumbling block at going your own way when gardening indoors, but if you wish to have the least amount of trouble, enjoy the beauty of these "indestructibles."

The indestructibles—the 10 easiest to grow house plants

CHINESE EVERGREEN—*(Alglao-mema modestum, A. simplex)* This one's near the top of the list for indestructibility. Has large, glossy, dark green leaves, reaches a height of two to three feet. Tolerates low light situations. Keep soil moist.

CAST IRON PLANT—*(Aspidistra elatior)* One of the original "indestructibles"; lives up to its common name. Particularly good in shady corners where nothing else will grow; will also grow in sunny locations. Dark green, shiny leaves which grow to 2 feet. Keep soil evenly moist.

SPIDER PLANT—*(Chlorophytum elatum)* Good hanging plant. Small plants form at ends of long swooping stems from the mother plant. Likes a warm location; good to hang in front of a window.

DRACAENA—There are many species in the Dracaena family, all of them quite rugged. Some varieties will grow to 15 feet or more, resembling a thick-leafed palm.

FICUS—Rubber Plant and Figs— An old standby—does best in good light, but not direct sun. Keep moist, and these plants will grow to over six feet.

PHILODENDRON—Many species— large glossy leaves have a tropical effect. Tolerates most light conditions, grows large unless pruned.

GRAPE IVY—*(Cissus)* Good for hanging baskets, or to climb up a wall. Tolerates a wide range of light conditions. Keep soil on the moist side.

UMBRELLA TREE—*(Brassaia* or schefflera) Will grow to height of 6 feet, with spreading shiny leaves. Likes good light, but not direct sun. Keep soil evenly moist.

ARROWHEAD PLANT—*(Syngonium* or nephytis) Can be grown as a climber or pinched back to form a more bushy plant. Tolerates most light conditions, likes even moisture. Leaves shaped like arrowheads, variegated.

PIGGY-BACK PLANT—*(Tolmiea menziesii)* Irregular-shaped, hairy leaves. When mature can be used as a hanging plant. Likes moist soil, and indirect light.

These ferns are humidity lovers and enjoy frequent mistings with a squeeze bottle sprayer. The large fronds on the right belong to the Polypodium; *the remainder are different kinds of* Adiantum *or maidenhairs.*

A sunken garden planted at the end of a Florida living room, complete with a running fountain. Many of the plants are grown directly in the soil; others are in containers for indoor/outdoor mobility to give variety and maintain health.

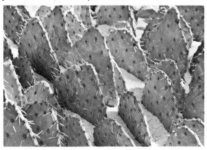

Representatives of the Euphorbias, *succulents which resemble many cactus species, but will tolerate less light. Also included in this family is the Christmas poinsettia.*

Succulents make attractive desertscapes. Be sure to provide drainage in the dish.

The pony tail palm, Beaucarnia recurvata, stores water in its large swollen woody base. It enjoys mistings with tepid water frequently and grows in a semi-shady location. Sometimes called Mexican bottle plant; grows to large tree.

Commercial grown Opuntias await cross country shipments to local retailers.

The golden barrel Notocactus, top, is available in 2½ inch pots to giant aged specimens. Rebutia, lower photo, is encircled with brightly colored flowers in the summer. Both of these are good species for beginning cactus hobbyist.

Cactus and succulents...

A new world to conquer

Cactus are so different from other plants that some botanists suggest they might have been brought from another planet. Some 10,000 plants including all the cactus, are catalogued as succulents—plants with the ability to store water in stems and leaves for use during periods of drought. This reservoir of water causes the odd shapes which can be appreciated for their structural form.

Hot, arid deserts are not the only homes for succulents. They are found all over the world—in jungles, along cool, shady streams and on mountains where they are forced to endure strong, cold winds. All these native habitats have periods of rain followed by drought. Nature has endowed succulents with unusual abilities to thrive under the most severe conditions. For this reason they can stand more neglect than almost any other form of plant life.

In choosing cactus and other succulents it is important to know what part of the world the plant comes from and the kind of atmosphere it likes. Determine your growing conditions and select suitable plants.

As a stepping stone into this hobby, you may want to consult specialized books on the subject or secure literature from professional groups. The Cactus and Succulent Society of America offers a monthly journal with up-to-the-minute information for members. Automatic membership is given when you order the *Cactus and Succulent Journal* ($10. per year), 1593 Los Canoas Road, Santa Barbara, California 93105.

Millions of succulents are produced by California commercial growers using one single growing mix for hundreds of types of plants. The "soil" mix used is the U.C. type. See page 11 for formula. The growers found, as many cactus and succulent gardeners have found, that shifting mixes to suit various types of plants was not necessary. The important quality that the mix must furnish is fast drainage.

Growers are finding that some of the standard ingredients of the mix are hard to come by and changes have to be made in the organic matter used. But whatever the change the mix must have good aeration and fast drainage.

Hobbyists, of course, have their own ideas about soil mixes but a good solution for the home grower is the purchase of pre-packaged mixes. Quite a few are marketed for cactus and other succulents.

Some western growers solved the problem of soil spillage in air shipments to the east by growing plants in blocks of a mixture of building plaster and peat moss. Amazingly the plants survive for several years although their growth is stunted.

Advice from a true hobbyist

We talked to an avid succulent collector for advice on beginning a collection. Her main point was "Leave them alone! Don't kill them with too much attention. Given half a chance they will thrive. Just provide good drainage and water only when necessary. A general rule is to water well, then after soil becomes dry, wait one or two days before watering again. Find the right atmosphere for the plant. If a plant isn't doing well in sunlight, move it to sheltered light. Many succulents thrive and bloom in shade and humidity, contrary to most people's idea. Move a plant around until you find a spot it likes, even if it's an attic or a basement.

"Don't waste money on cheap plants. Buy good ones from legitimate growers or start your own from slips of plants belonging to friends. Succulents propagate easily. Place the slips in loose, sterile soil."

An easy group of succulents to grow are the *Euphorbias*. Make sure the cuttings of euphorbias just kiss the soil or place clumps of earth gently around them. Don't water any succulent cutting or transplant for at least a week. Sprinkle lightly with water at first. Heavy watering will cause "damping off" or rot to young succulents.

When moving succulents from indoors to outdoors, or vice versa, make the transition gradually. Expose to stronger or lesser light for a few hours per day.

Many of the plants shown on these pages are among the more interesting varieties which were considered collector's items until recently. The current interest in succulents has forced the commercial grower to make them available.

Plants shown here were selected for appearance, suitable size for containers, flowering habits, ease of culture and commercial availability. All grow in the temperature and normally dry humidity of the average house in sunny to semi-sunny locations.

Many succulents make good hanging baskets. Shown here are three of the showiest kinds. Rhipsalis, *upper left, is the humidity and sheltered light loving mistletoe cactus from tropical jungles. The orchid cactus,* Epiphyllum, *shown lower left, produces brilliant water-lily type flowers.* Senecio rowelayanus, *the popular string-of-pearls, is easy to grow bearing tiny white blooms. Hanging succulents love warm temperatures near the ceiling.*

Living stones or Lithrops, *upper left, are difficult to distinguish from the ceramic planter. In summer a colorful bloom appears between the split leaves.* Faucaria, *upper right, is commonly called tigers jaws because of toothlike edges.* Sedum, *such as the one shown in the lower left, make excellent ground covers in large plantings. Exotic blooms grow on the rosette shaped* Echiveria. *Its foliage comes in a wide range of colors and textures.*

An or a herb (depending on how you treat the "h") doesn't know it's a herb.

The special attention given to herbs as a class of plants is due to the need for directions in use rather than how-to-grow. Many are as easy to grow as any plant in the garden.

A whimsical touch is shown in the Mexican pottery planting of parsley.

Potted herbs make an easy transition from outdoors to the kitchen or vice versa.

We consider here ten herbs—most all are used frequently in the kitchen. All are used in the green leaf stage. Most of them can summer in the garden and, if potted up in the fall, will winter in the kitchen. All will grow bushier with frequent picking of fresh leaves.

The ten are: sweet basil, chives, dill, sweet marjoram, mint, oregano, parsley, sage, tarragon and thyme.

A planter box or special bed near the kitchen will take care of 6 or more of your choice. Or grow herbs in pots for easy transition from outdoors to kitchen. Only dill is better treated exclusively as a garden plant.

Sweet Basil—is an easy to grow annual, 1-2 feet high with leafy, light-green foliage. Spikelets of tiny flowers are white and often tinged with lavender. A spicy herb with a slight taste of pepper. "Dark Opal" is an ornamental variety of sweet basil, with dark purple-bronze foliage and small lavender flowers. Has a much milder flavor than other basils.

Bush Basil—is a compact form of sweet basil growing to 6-12 inches.

GROWING TIPS. Sow seeds in place after last frost, or start plants indoors and transplant. They like full sun; pinch tips to promote bushier, more compact growth.

Chives—have fine, grass-like blades which have a delicate onion flavor. It is a hardy perennial, willing to be clipped almost continuously. If not clipped chives produces pompoms of lavender flowers above their grass-like leaves every spring.

Attractive as a border plant or indoors in pots. You can freeze surplus with little loss in flavor.

Dill—is an annual that grows to 2-4 feet. Lacy light green leaves and tiny greenish-yellow flowers appear in

An herb clock with sundial shows a creative planting with herbs sectionalized for easy culture and harvesting. Small gardens use a reduced version.

Knot gardens of herbs can be planted in infinite patterns. This practice used in colonial gardens is adaptable to the contemporary gardener.

Lacy flowers of the dill plant tower above feathery foliage. Both the weedy leaves and seed heads are used in cooking.

Flowering chives add color to herb garden as a bonus to their excellent seasoning.

Herbs enjoy the same culture as most vegetables and make good garden companions.

parasol shaped clusters. Produces large amount of seeds.

GROWING TIPS. Sow seed in place in spring in a sunny location. You may have to stake tall, growing plants. Both the seeds and the dill weed (the leafy part) get wide use in the kitchen.

Sweet Marjoram—is a perennial, but is treated as an annual in all but the mildest winter area. It is an attractive bushy plant and does well in containers. Grows 1-2 feet high with small oval leaves and small clusters of white to pale lilac flowers.

Mint—there are many varieties of mint, but Spearmint is the most common garden variety and has the widest range of uses in the kitchen. Spearmint grows to a height of 1 to 2 feet and has reddish stems and crinkly pointed leaves.

GROWING TIPS. Start with divisions rather than seed. Grown in containers, even when planted in the soil, because of its spreading nature and invasive root system. Takes sun or shade and tolerates continuously moist soil. Cut flowering stalks before they go to seed.

Oregano—is a first cousin to sweet marjoram, often called wild or winter marjoram. A hardy perennial and good container plant, oregano forms a leafy shrub-like plant 2-2½ feet tall.

GROWING TIPS. Grow from seeds or divisions. Seeds germinate slowly, so starting seeds indoors helps assure good first-season growth. Cutting back flowers will stimulate growth of foliage. Replant when plants become woody in 3 to 4 years.

Parsley—today most gardeners and cooks are familiar with parsley for its use in the garden and in the kitchen. What the gardener and the good cook should know are the different varieties of parsley.

'Moss Curled' or 'Triple Curled.' Leaves are finely cut and deeply curled. Excellent for garnishing and culinary decoration. 'Deep Green' and 'Evergreen' varieties are similar to 'Moss Curled.'

'Plain or Single.' Bright green flat leaves are deeply cut but not curled. Standard variety for flavoring.

'Dark Green *Italien.*' A flat leafed type. Heavy, glossy, medium dark green leaves of strong flavor. More attractive than 'Plain.'

Sage—is a shrublike perennial from 1 to 2 feet tall. Greyish-green oblong leaves heavily veined. Purple flowers appear on tall spikes. *Variegated varieties* available having leaves marked with tints of yellow (golden sage); reddish purple (purple sage) and white and deep red (tricolor sage). Makes a handsome low hedge around vegetable or herb gardens.

GROWING TIPS. Start from seed or cuttings. Seeds are slow to start, so it's best to start them indoors and transplant. Give them full sun. Plants eventually become woody and should be renewed every 3 to 4 years.

Tarragon—is a perennial herb that will hold its own in a flower border and is most attractive in pots. It takes partial shade and grows to a height of 2 feet. Fine, dark green leaves have pointed tips. Extremely small whitish-green flowers are tightly clustered. Leaves are most flavorful when picked pre-bloom or just as the blooming begins.

Common Thyme—also called garden thyme, is a perennial, shrublike plant from 8 to 12 inches high. Has slender woody branches and tiny grey-green leaves, and loose spikes of purplish flowers. Though there are many varieties of thyme, the common thyme is recognized as the most flavorful.

Meet the competition— How much damage can a plant take?

There's competition for your crops in all stages of plant growth from birds, squirrels, gophers, mice, rabbits, insects, diseases, not to mention the ways the human animal has of hindering the natural growth of plants.

The gardener doesn't grow a plant. A plant grows by itself and it is up to the gardener to see that it has the environment to grow in. The competition to corn or lettuce plants, for example, may be another corn or lettuce plant. Failure to thin plants to the proper distance in the row has the same effect as failure to pull weeds between plants.

The natural destiny of all plants is to produce seeds. With such familiar root crops as carrots, beets and radishes, the gardener aborts the natural process and harvests the vegetable in its food storage cycle. The continuous harvesting of cucumbers and squash is only possible when the gardener keeps the plant out of the seed-ripening stage by removing over-sized fruits.

Meeting the competition, in whatever form it takes, is an important part of gardening—one which a good gardener never ignores.

Birds

Our feathered friends are a joy to hear and watch, however they can wreak havoc in the garden. Many vegetable seedlings and most fruits need protection from bird damage. Here are several solutions to the problem of birds.

If you wish to make your own protection, the following good ideas:

I made a cover of aluminum fly screen. Built portable frames 14 inches wide and 7 inches high and 9 feet long for my peas and beans and smaller ones 7 inches wide for carrots, beets and lettuce. I store them in the winter and bring them out for the first seed sowing. They're very simple.

Length should be ½, ⅓ or ¼ the length of a full row. Just staple the wire to frame. A heavy stapling gun is

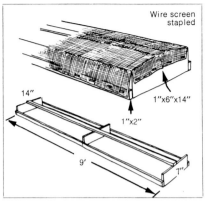

ideal and very fast. The 7-inch height is adequate. After plants are 6 inches tall, birds don't do much damage. The first year we used 1-inch mesh chicken wire. It didn't stop the mice. Small birds squeezed through and couldn't get out again. No trouble after covering with the aluminum fly screen.

A cone of wire screen or plastic hardware cloth tacked to a stake keeps birds off a plant as well as giving some wind and frost protection.

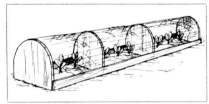

Plastic mesh is available in sizes from 4½ x36 feet to 9x200 feet, enough to cover a row crop or an entire tree. It is reusable many times and can be staked and stretched over newly planted corn, peas, and beans, as well as keeping birds from enjoying the fruit on strawberry plants, tomato plants, grape vines and fruit trees.

BAGGING. In areas where there is trouble with birds eating the kernels on the tip of the ear of corn, the problem can be solved by slipping a paper bag over each ear after it's pollinated. Large clusters of grapes can be protected from yellow jackets

and birds by tying a plastic bag around the cluster.

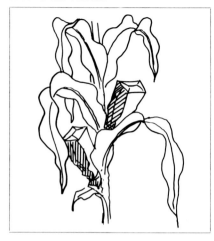

Gardeners try all sorts of things to discourage birds: "My son has a project of about 20 acres of sweet corn and he is using all kinds of exploders to scare the birds. If you are in a populated area, the exploders or cannons aren't very popular with the natives since you start them at daylight and keep them running until just about dark."

Gophers

Anyone who has gardened with a family of gophers knows the frustration of watching a row of plants disappear. Here are two solutions offered by gardeners:

"Two families of gophers practically ruined our garden last year. This year we have gopher-proofed one section by building a 12-inch deep raised bed and lining the bottom of the bed with ½-inch mesh wire."

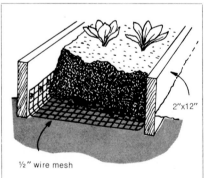

Another gardener plants in plastic cans, with holes in the bottom, sunk into the soil so that the main roots cannot be attacked.

Man's inhumanity to plants

When a plant leaves the nursery it's ready to grow. So if it fails, you can be pretty sure that the gardener has somehow goofed in the first weeks of his ownership. The following are some of the things nurserymen would like good gardeners to be aware of—

Don't have the can cut unless you are going to plant the shrub or tree right away. A can that has been cut is almost impossible to water properly.

If you take a large tree or shrub home, don't let it stick out a car window or trunk without wrapping it first with a piece of cloth or similar material. A plant will be rapidly wind-burned if left unprotected speeding down the highway at 55 miles an hour.

Don't pick a container plant up by the trunk or stem—the roots may not be well established.

If a plant won't come out of a metal can easily at planting time, *cut* the can with a pair of tin snips or can cutters—don't knock the can about trying to get the plant out.

Don't put an 8 foot tree into a compact car—have it delivered—both you and your new tree will benefit.

Most nurserymen worry about their customers and hate to see transplants of tomatoes, peppers and eggplants going out when the weather is too cold and uncertain for successful growth. But once the spring urge strikes there seems to be no use warning customers that these warm weather crops should not be planted until the weather warms.

More plants are being grown in plastic containers or tapered cans which do not have to be cut to get the plants out. Don't try to yank a plant out of the container. Hold the plant in place at the top of the root ball, gently jar the edge of the container and the plant should slip out easily, especially if it has been watered beforehand.

It may only take a day or two for wind and sun to pull water out of a newly planted root ball, even when the surrounding soil is wet. Make

sure that the ball stays moist while the roots are spreading out beyond it. Build a small temporary basin, a little larger than the root system. Water every other day for the first 10 days in hot weather.

Spacing

Vegetable specialist, Raymond Sheldrake of Cornell University has this to say about spacing vegetables:

"Many gardeners find it difficult to thin out vegetable seedlings, but actually too many seedlings in a row can act just like weeds. This commonly occurs when people try to grow head lettuce, or even leaf lettuce or sweet corn, carrots, beets, radishes and spinach. All of these seeds come up, and these plants have got to have room if they're going to develop into good quality vegetables.

"Gardeners sometimes forget that root crops such as beets and carrots need leaf space as well as root space. If the leaf doesn't have a chance to develop fully, the beet won't either.

"Many people wonder why their sweet corn only produces little nubbins of ears and not the nice big ears with good flag leaves like you see on road stands. The trouble is generally in spacing.

"Most sweet corn varieties should be 8 to 12 inches apart between each stalk and the rows should be 36 inches apart. I see many gardens with sweet corn 1 or 2 inches apart and the poor plants can't possibly produce good ears.

"On the subject of melons—we grow all of our melons in 6 to 8 foot rows, and space plants 2 to 3 feet apart. We get so much vine growth, that if we plant them too close, we get nothing but a bunch of vines and very small melons.

"So go out in the garden and take a look to see if the carrots or beets or lettuce or radishes are too close. If they are just reach in there and thin them out so they have room to grow."

Disease resistance

Disease resistance may be an essential factor to look for when planting some vegetables. There are localities where many vegetables such as tomatoes and cucumbers can be grown with little attention to disease problems. There are places where scab, mosaic, powdery mildew, downy mildew, anthracnose, and verticillium and fusarium wilt will put an end to your hopes for a crop. If you have had trouble growing cucumbers, tomatoes or other vegetables bothered by the above diseases, try a disease resistant variety.

The following vegetables are troubled with the diseases listed:

Tomatoes—Fusarium, verticillium.
Cucumbers—Scab, mosaic, downy mildew, powdery mildew, anthracnose.

Muskmelon—Fusarium, powdery mildew.

Snap beans—Mosaic, powdery mildew, root rot.

Cabbage—Virus Yellows

Spinach—Blight, blue mold, downy mildew, mosaic.

See pages 35 and 38 for varieties bred for disease resistance.

Diseases and rotation

Controlling diseases by rotation of crops is good and often-repeated advice in all garden literature. Sometimes it is excellent advice that is hard to follow.

When you are told that "strawberries should never be planted in soil in which tomatoes have been grown" and you're working at a ten foot square garden, what do you do? One gardener we know fills large containers having ample drainage with new soil to meet the needs of the crop he intends to grow and sets them in the ground. Apparently such planting keeps diseases from spreading into the new soil.

If you have plenty of room, rotation is most effective when the garden site is changed every few years. Rotating crops within the garden so that the same crop does not occupy the same space year after year will help some.

Below is one gardener's system of rotating his crops:

My system of rotation is very simple. Divide the garden into quarters. Plant what was in quarter #1 this year and quarter #2 next year, etc.

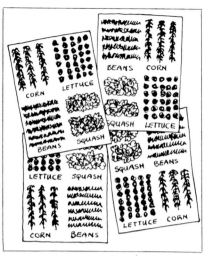

Are you your gardens worst enemy?

Besides having to put up with animals, insects and diseases, a garden sometimes suffers from the hand of the gardener himself. Good gardeners are aware that trees and plants have a life of their own. A gardener who respects his trees and plants doesn't knock the bark off a tree trunk with the lawn mower, or pound nails into a tree's side. The good gardener also makes sure that a tree isn't growing into a tree-tie that has become too tight. When rototilling he doesn't cut through the roots of nearby plants, and when hoeing he keeps the hoe close to his toe, scraping instead of chopping.

Good gardeners avoid the frustration of growing vegetables by accepting the natural rhythm of plant growth rather than trying to make plants fit their rhythm. Spring fever in the first warm days of the season is not the best guide for when to plant. The full enjoyment of the vegetable garden comes when you are in step with beets, lettuce, beans and all the vegetables you grow.

Check the planting chart on pages 88-90. Are the vegetables you are thinking about in the cool-season or warm-season group? Some of the cool-weather crops may need to be planted before you feel like gardening.

"Cool-season" means more than that the vegetables can be planted early. The quality, the good taste of peas and beets, for example, depends on the right temperatures in which they ripen. The first picking of garden peas and the harvest of beets are the great ones.

Waiting for the soil to warm up for the planting of beans and corn or night temperatures to rise for setting out transplants of tomatoes may seem like nonsense on the first warm day of spring, but if the soil temperature is below 55°, beans will rot and tomatoes just sit and sulk. Lima seeds are likely to rot if the soil is below 62°.

The length of day influences the growth habit of several annual vegetables. Spinach and Chinese cabbage are notorious examples. As days lengthen beyond the 12 hour day and 12 hour night of the vernal equinox they get a signal that it's time to flower. Rising temperatures along with the longer days play a part in this flowering habit. Gardeners learn about the influence of day length by crops "bolting" to seed before they are ready to harvest.

Gardeners who have tried to grow Chinese cabbage in the spring rate it among the difficult-to-grow vegetables. When grown to mature in the short days of fall, it is as easy to grow as any vegetable.

Premature flowering also occurs in lettuce but the cause is more that of hot weather than day length. The choice of varieties to fit the season is all important. Seed packet descriptions will say if the lettuce is a bolting-resistant variety or not.

Gardeners in short season climates get along with nature and grow vegetables that normally require a long warm growing season by planting "early" varieties.

To these gardeners the word "early" means more than early. It means that the vegetable will grow and produce a crop with less total summer heat than the later maturing varieties.

You might be the stumbling block

The next best thing from removing yourself from the garden is a check-up on your gardening habits.

The habit of cleanliness

The garden that is always clean and neat suffers less damage from diseases than a sloppy one. When a crop is harvested all the vines, leaves, and fruit are cleaned up and spread on the compost pile or spaded under. There's never a weed over two weeks old. In a really clean garden an infected plant stands out and is quickly removed and destroyed. For the gardener with the cleanliness habit only a healthy plant is a "clean plant" and he waters and fertilizes to make it so.

Good garden habits

The gardeners who enjoy taking care of that "ounce of prevention" are the successful ones. They can't stay away from the garden when the first sprouts are about to break through. Weeds, no more than an inch high are pulled and the soil checked for crusting over the seed row.

When we tallied the reasons why gardens fail, among the friends of our panel members, the failure to get at the first weeding job was number one.

The good gardener never lets the soil dry out but he waters as infrequently as possible. He looks beneath the surface of the soil. He learns the difference between a moist soil and a wet soil.

Gardeners who talk with plants or at least look at them with a questioning eye, are likely to have a healthy, beautiful garden. They are aware of the first signs of trouble and in time to prevent big trouble.

The Spoilers

To prevent insects from damaging plant growth and to protect your food supply are the main reasons for spraying and dusting. How much damage can the plant take? It depends upon the purpose of the plant. Deciduous shade trees are able to get along with a loss of 10 to 20 percent of its foliage to chewing insects. Fruit and nut trees on the other hand cannot produce their quota with such a loss of leaves and, of course, the fruits and nuts must be protected.

Here are some of the insect competitors you're likely to meet up with:

Tomato russet mite

You need a 20-power hand lens to see the russet mite (it's white and pear-shaped) but the damage is visible. First, the lower stems become bronze or russet, then the bronzing spreads up the plant, giving it a smoked appearance. To stop damage, dust or spray with a garden sulfer and repeat as necessary. Check the label.

Strawberry root weevil

Tell tale signs of weevils are notching of the foliage. The strawberry root weevil prefers azalea, rhododendron, camellia and primrose.

Adults emerge from the soil during late May and June and lay eggs around crown of plants. Larvae move down and feed on roots.

To prevent damage before planting, drench soil with Chlordane. Mix it into the top 4 inches of soil. Or with established plants spray generously at 2 tablespoons Chlordane per gallon of water around base of plants and work it into the soil.

Look what happened to my radishes

When you're trying to control insects, you can't always wait for the damage to show up. This is definitely true with soil insects. So many gardeners have failures with radishes and onions, due to soil maggots, that prevention seems the only wise thing to do. There are three methods you can use:

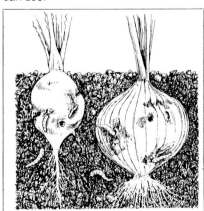

You can apply Diazinon soil and foliage dust to the entire garden area and work it into the soil before planting, or you can simply apply the dust in the furrow as the seed is planted, or you can use liquid Diazinon to put in the planting holes of vegetables as you set them out. Be sure to read and follow label directions.

Radishes seem to be the favorite food of these maggots, but onions may be attacked, as well as the roots of all the members of the cabbage family.

Corn earworm

Prevent damage from corn earworm by spraying or dusting silks with Sevin spray or dust. Apply 1, 4 and 7 days after silks appear. Repeat weekly until silks are brown.

Another borer, the European corn borer damages both stalks and ears from base or side. When ear shoots form, spray them in center of leaf whorls with Sevin spray. Repeat at least 3 times at 5-day intervals. Apply spray until runoff occurs at base of plant.

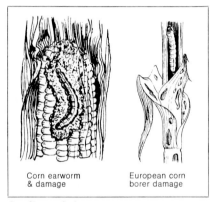

Corn earworm & damage   European corn borer damage

Snails and slugs— They lurk in the darkness

These slimy night feeders must have moisture to live. They are a major problem where moisture and cool, humid, cloudy weather prevails. They do their damage at night and hide during the day so that their presence is often unsuspected. Snails and slugs are capable of making a harvest overnight of newly set out transplants and seedlings.

It's wise to scatter a barrier of slug and snail bait around vegetable plantings to protect tender young seedlings.

In other areas where these invaders are a problem, broadcast slug and snail bait over a wide area to rid the garden of their damage.

These are some of the "good guys"—the beneficial insects that prey on aphids, mites, caterpillars, bugs and other harmful insects. If you should find them in your garden welcome them and protect them as the friends they are.

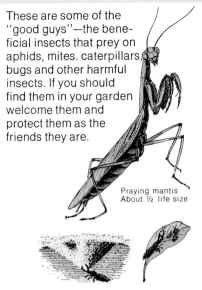

Praying mantis About ½ life size

The larvae of some lacewings build cone-shaped "ant-lion" pits commonly seen in dry places. They wait at the bottom for insects. Larvae of other lacewings feed on aphids and are called "aphid-lions."

Lacewing adult enlarged about 2x

Here are only two of some 350 species of Ladybird beetles found throughout the world. Both larvae and adults have big appetites and eat many aphids each day.

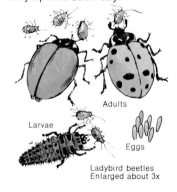

Adults

Larvae   Eggs

Ladybird beetles Enlarged about 3x

Ground beetles and tiger beetles feed on many harmful insects. They search for prey in the litter and debris on the ground.

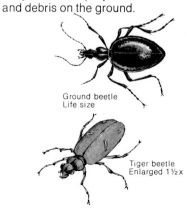

Ground beetle Life size

Tiger beetle Enlarged 1½x

Aphids

Aphids come in several assorted colors and sizes to suck plant juices, stunt growth, pucker and curl leaves, cause formation of galls, deform buds and flowers, and make a nuisance of themselves around the garden. All secrete honey-dew which attracts ants and is a medium for the growth of black sooty mold fungus.

HOSTS: All plants.
CONTROLS: Diazinon, Malathion, Sevin

Scale Insects

Scale are divided into two groups, armored and soft. Armored scale live beneath an outer shell of molted skins and waxy secretions. The soft scale shell is an integral part of the scale like the shell of a turtle, and though called "soft" is often as hard as armored scale. Soft scale usually secrete honey-dew, causing unsightly blackening of foliage and sticky drippings on cars and walks beneath.

A scale's mouth is a needle-like tube that uncoils 6-7 times as long as his body, reaching deep into plant tissue to suck juices, reducing plant vitality. Foliage pales, leaves or needles drop prematurely.

Heavy infestations may kill branches, sometimes entire tree or shrub.

Except when in their "crawler stage," scales are immobile, protected from predators and most insecticides by their shell.

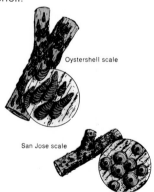

SAN JOSE SCALE. Encrusts bark and fruit. HOSTS: Flowering fruit trees, pyracantha, cotoneaster, elm, ash, and many others.
OYSTERSHELL SCALE. Encrusts twigs and branches. HOSTS: Flowering fruit trees, dogwood, boxwood, ash, holly, viburnum, birch, and poplar.

LECANIUM SCALE. Large, shiny brown. HOSTS: Arborvitae, yew, flowering fruit, oak, maple, and others.
EUROPEAN ELM SCALE. Encrusts bark, especially in forks and crotches.
HOSTS: Elms, of all ages.

BROWN SOFT SCALE. Usually mimics color of host. Infects leaves and soft stems. HOSTS: Camellia, gardenia, holly, oleander, and many others. CONTROLS: Diazinon (Crawlers), Malathion, Sevin, Dormant Oil Spray

Mites

Mites are not really insects. They are in the class arachnida with spiders, ticks, and scorpions. Many species damage plants by sucking sap from lower leaf surfaces. Top surface of damaged leaf turns pale or yellow, becomes covered with tiny yellow specks. Turn over suspicious looking leaves— look for small webs, many dark specks of excrement and discarded skins, and mites themselves. Use a hand lens.

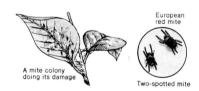

Mites that attack leafy plants become more active in hot weather. Those that damage conifers start in the cool of early spring. HOSTS: Many flowers; cucumbers and melons; ivy, oak, elm, spruce, fir, pine, and many others. CONTROLS: Diazinon, Malathion, Dormant Oil Spray

Beetles

This is a huge and diverse group of insects containing many beneficial insects as well as those that are destructive. Try never to harm ladybird beetles (ladybugs), or black ground beetles. They are predaceous and feed on aphids, grubs, and other harmful insects. The most destructive beetles are illustrated here.

Damage varies in almost as many ways as there are beetles. The larva of the elm leaf beetle eat everything but the veins of leaves, weakens trees and makes them fair game for the elm bark beetle which carries spores of the Dutch elm disease fungus. Flea beetles give leaves of young plants a shot-hole pattern and spreads disease causing virus. The larva of the striped cucumber beetle feeds on the roots of cucumbers, muskmelons, and winter squash while the adults feed on the leaves and blossoms of many plants. These beetles double their damage by spreading such diseases as bacterial wilt and cucumber mosaic.

CONTROLS: Diazinon, Malathion, Sevin

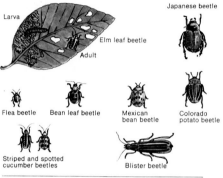

True Bugs

To most people, any insect is a bug. To a gardener, "bugs" are a sub-order of insects, generally unpleasant, destructive, and difficult to control. Bugs have an incomplete metamorphosis—nymphs resemble adults, but are smaller and lack wings.

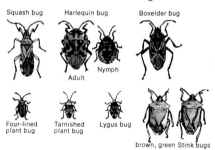

As bugs suck juices, many inject a toxin causing unsightly spots and wilting. HOSTS: General feeder throughout the garden. CONTROLS: Diazinon, Malathion, Sevin

Mealybugs

Close relatives of scale, have soft segmented bodies up to ¼" long, covered with powdery white wax that extends in filaments beyond the body. May occur singly or in groups on twigs and undersides of branches, mostly in crotches. Injury is accomplished by sucking sap and secreting large amounts of honey-dew. Tend to inhabit interior of plant, hidden areas where they may go unnoticed until loss of color, wilting, and even death of part or all of plant results.

HOSTS: Gardenias, amaryllus, camellia, catalpa, cineraria, cycas, crotons, ivy, lantana, oleander, magnolia—also likes soft-stemmed plants: coleus, begonias, geraniums and ferns.
CONTROLS: Diazinon, Malathion, Dormant Oil Spray

Leaf Miners

The larvae of several kinds of flies, midges and moths lay eggs on or within leaves. When eggs hatch, they feed inside, between the leaf surfaces creating ugly blotches or serpentine trails.

Serpentine mine on holly

Blotch mine on birch

Leaf Miners attack conifers as well as leafy plants. HOSTS: Spruce, white fir, pine, arborvitae; flowering cherry, azalea, aspen, birch, holly, and other trees; many flowers.
CONTROLS: Diazinon, Sevin

Leafhoppers

Leafhoppers are small, ⅛″-½″ long, wedge-shaped insects with piercing-sucking mouthparts. They feed on all kinds of plants and trees, usually sucking sap from the undersides of leaves, causing loss of color, a stippled, wilted appearance, and a general loss of health and vigor. Some species inject a toxic substance as they feed, causing a wilting of leaves. Leafhoppers are also carriers of many plant virus diseases.

Leafhoppers are easily seen—hop away quickly when disturbed. HOSTS: General feeder on all plants.
CONTROLS: Diazinon, Malathion

Thrips

Thrips scrape and scar foliage, feed inside buds so flowers are deformed or fail to open. They are tiny, barely visible without a lens. Usually discovered only when damage is apparent. Can be seen slithering for cover when infested flower is examined or shaken over paper.

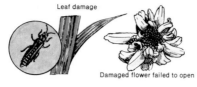

Leaf damage

Damaged flower failed to open

Knowledge of life cycle is relatively useless. They enter the garden in massive flights as adults. HOSTS: Shasta daisies, gladiolus, roses, and others.
CONTROLS: Diazinon, Malathion, Sevin

Whiteflies

Adult whiteflies are small, 1/16″ long, wedge-shaped, pure white. Fly like little clouds of snowflakes when disturbed. Nymphs do the damage—scale-like, flat, oval, pale green, brown or black depending on species. Some have white waxy fringe. Suck juices from underside of leaves, secrete honey-dew. Infested leaves become pale, mottled, may turn yellow and die.

An all-year pest in warm-winter areas; summer pest where winters are cold. HOSTS: Especially serious on tomatoes, beans, ixora, gardenia, and privet. Infests many others.
CONTROLS: Diazinon, Malathion, Dormant Oil Spray (Larvae)

Caterpillars & Worms

Most of these are the larva of moths and butterflies. They come in all sizes and colors, naked and hairy, some decorated with tufts or spines. All feed on foliage. Many have a spinneret for making silk thread. They have special names based on their appearance, hosts, or way of life—leafrollers, bagworms, hornworms, pickleworms, leaf skeletonizers, and many others.

Leaf tier

Leaf roller

LEAF ROLLERS AND TIERS. Caterpillars that feed inside rolled or tied-together leaves. HOSTS: Basswood, canna, elm, honeylocust, honeysuckle, locust, oak, redbud, willow, and others.

Tussock moth larva

Larva of the notorious TUSSOCK MOTH feeds on many deciduous shade trees skeletonizing the leaves. In the East the first generation feeds from April to June, the second in August and September.

Banded woolybear

BANDED WOOLYBEAR is the larva of the tiger moth. Touch him and he rolls in a ball. Feeds on many garden plants.

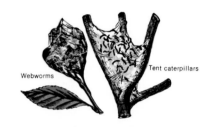

Webworms   Tent caterpillars

WEBWORMS AND TENT CATERPILLARS. Some build unsightly "tents" in forks or crotches of trees and crawl from them to feed. Others web together needles or leaves (usually at the ends of branches) and feed beneath the webs. HOSTS: Many trees and shrubs.

Cankerworms

LOOPERS, INCHWORMS, MEASURING WORMS, AND CANKERWORMS. There are many kinds that all have the same movement. They double or loop when they crawl. On trees they feed on new foliage in spring and are known as cankerworms. In the vegetable garden the cabbage looper eats ragged holes in the leaves of cabbage and lettuce.

Hornworm

HORNWORM is big, 2½ to 3 inches long and has a big appetite. It is most destructive on tomatoes. Leaves seem to disappear overnight.
CATERPILLARS & WORMS
CONTROLS: Diazinon, Sevin

How to start at the top

If you take advantage of the services offered through your local County Agricultural or Extension Agent you'll have access to enough information to become a successful, "seasoned" gardener on your first try.

The Cooperative Extension Service is a storehouse of the latest "tried and true" localized information for the home gardener. As the name implies, the Cooperative Extension Service is a *cooperative* effort of the United States Department of Agriculture and each state university. The latest findings and developments in the field of agriculture, fruit and nut crops, and horticulture from the USDA and university cooperating experiment stations flows, where it applies locally, into the office of the *Cooperative* County Extension Service.

There are 3,150 Extension Service Offices across the country—one in practically every county. One of the aims of the County Extension Agent is to put the results and findings of all the experiments and trials in the hands of the home gardener, but *you* have to ask for it.

What's in a name?

Unfortunately there isn't a standardized name for the "County Agent" or the "Cooperative Extension Service" used consistently throughout the states (see page 79). If you don't know who your County Agent is, the key is to look in the phone book under the name of your county for the Cooperative Extension Service, or to check in the yellow pages under the County Government Offices. If all else fails, you can write to your state university and request a list of County Extension Offices; they'll be happy to furnish the information.

The Extension Service changes

The change in the Extension Service is apparent in the changes being made in the names of the County Agent; the word *agriculture* is being phased out in the name. The County Extension Agent is no longer just a County Agriculture Agent. Before acres of farm and orchard land gave way to suburbia the name "Farm Advisor" fit the function of the agent very well. In counties where the small farm is still alive and well, the "Farm Advisor" is still a good one, but in counties taken over by expanding cities, the farms change to home gardens and "gardens" in townhouses and high rise apartments.

Russell E. Hibbard, past president of the National Association of County Agents describes how the Cooperative Extension Service has kept up with the current demands:

"Today the image of the County Agricultural Agent has changed in the eyes of many people. No longer is he a person that primarily serves agriculture. The Extension Program has always been a dynamic program changing as the educational needs of society have dictated.

"In recent times, the 4-H and homemaking programs have spread rapidly to serve our total population. The County Agent has specialized not only to serve agriculture but our total environment as well. The Colleges of Agriculture, his supporting source of information, have grown to include specialists in areas of Community Development and Natural Resources.

"Even more recently the Extension Agent has been called on to meet the educational needs of our inner cities. Special youth programs and an expanded nutrition program have been initiated."

For the home gardener this change means the campus of the state university has been extended to include interested gardeners everywhere. Not only the county office but the university can be an invaluable source of information on many subjects. On the following page we have listed the addresses of the state universities in this area. A letter to the office indicated of your state university, asking for a list of all available publications may bring you a surprisingly long list of bulletins, pamphlets and books.

Most of the publications listed are for distribution within the state, but we found a number of booklets and books priced for general sale. Such as:

The Cacti of Arizona, 218 pages with 150 illustrations from the University of Arizona Press. $6.95

Fundamentals of California Beekeeping, University of California, Manual 42, $1.00

Ficus—The Exotic Species, 360 pages. University of California. $4.30 ppd.

Government publications

Home gardeners everywhere also have a voluminous source of information in the United States government publications. To get acquainted with the available material write, Superintendent of Documents, Government Printing Office, Washington, D.C. for:

List of Available Publications of the U.S.D.A.,
Bulletin No. 11, 45¢.

Below is a sample of their publications:

Minigardens for Vegetables,
Home & Garden Bulletin No. 163, 15¢.

Growing Vegetables in the Home Garden,
Home and Garden Bulletin No. 202, 75¢.

Home Propagation of Ornamental Trees and Shrubs,
Home & Garden Bulletin No. 80, 10¢.

Indoor Gardens with Controlled Lighting,
Home & Garden Bulletin No. 187, 15¢.

Selecting and Growing House Plants,
Home & Garden Bulletin No. 82, 15¢.

Plant Hardiness and Zone Map,
Miscellaneous Publication No. 814, 25¢.

The city and suburban gardener should not expect a person to person interview when calling on the services of the County Extension Agent. The *office* of the County Extension Agent is the source of information. The Cooperative Extension Service is finding new ways to reach more home gardeners. Some Extension Services have even started a telephone information service—"Dial-a-Home & Garden Tip"—a one minute recorded message which give information of current interest to the home gardener.

In many areas the Extension Service has magnified its range by means of radio and newspaper coverage, as well as issuing monthly bulletins and newsletters. In some areas the Cooperative Extension Service sponsors monthly, informal classes on various phases of gardening, and in other counties the Extension Service has played an important part in establishing community gardens.

Information, please

For directory assistance, the following examples illustrate some of the ways the telephone companies list "The Cooperative Extension Service." In our brief survey of various city directories, the "County" listing appeared most frequently.

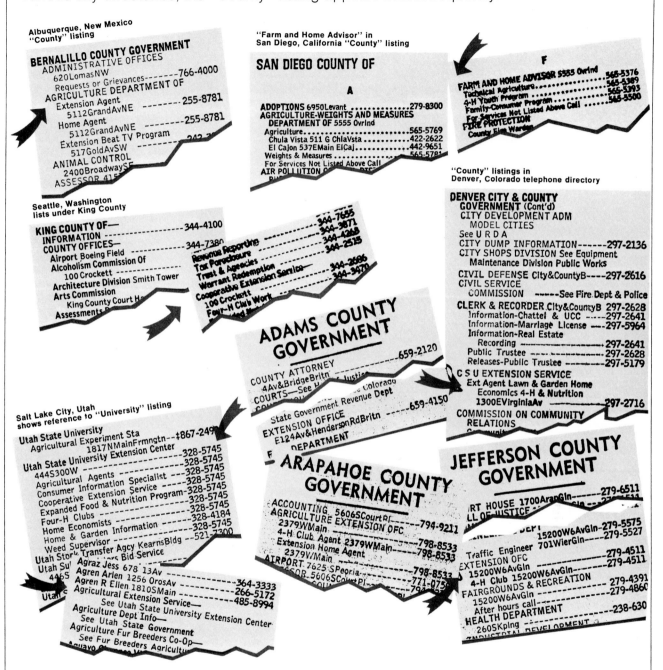

Albuquerque, New Mexico "County" listing

BERNALILLO COUNTY GOVERNMENT
ADMINISTRATIVE OFFICES
620 Lomas NW
Requests or Grievances--------766-4000
AGRICULTURE DEPARTMENT OF
Extension Agent
5112 Grand Av NE --------255-8781
Home Agent
5112 Grand Av NE --------255-8781
Extension Beat TV Program
517 Gold Av SW
ANIMAL CONTROL
2400 Broadway SE
ASSESSOR 41

"Farm and Home Advisor" in San Diego, California "County" listing

SAN DIEGO COUNTY OF

A

ADOPTIONS 6950 Levant 279-8300
AGRICULTURE-WEIGHTS AND MEASURES
DEPARTMENT OF 5555 Ovrlnd
Agriculture....................565-5769
Chula Vista 511 G ChlaVsta..........422-2622
El Cajon 537 E Main ElCaj...........442-9651
Weights & Measures..........565-578
For Services Not Listed Above Call
AIR POLLUTION

F
FARM AND HOME ADVISOR 5555 Ovrlnd........565-5376
Technical Agriculture...................565-5389
4-H Youth Program........................565-5393
Family-Consumer Program.................565-5500
For Services Not Listed Above Call
FIRE PROTECTION
County Fire Warden

Seattle, Washington lists under King County

KING COUNTY OF----------344-4100
INFORMATION
COUNTY OFFICES------------344-7380
Airport Boeing Field
Alcoholism Commission Of
100 Crockett
Architecture Division Smith Tower
Arts Commission
King County Court H
Assessments

Revenue Reporting............344-7655
Tax Foreclosure..............344-3871
Trust & Agencies.............344-4288
Warrant Redemption...........344-2515
Cooperative Extension Service......344-2686
100 Crockett.................344-3470
Four-H Club Work

"County" listings in Denver, Colorado telephone directory

DENVER CITY & COUNTY
GOVERNMENT (Cont'd)
CITY DEVELOPMENT ADM
MODEL CITIES
See U R D A
CITY DUMP INFORMATION------297-2136
CITY SHOPS DIVISION See Equipment
Maintenance Division Public Works
CIVIL DEFENSE City&CountyB----297-2616
CIVIL SERVICE
COMMISSION -----See Fire Dept & Police
CLERK & RECORDER City&CountyB 297-2628
Information-Chattel & UCC ----297-2641
Information-Marriage License ----297-5964
Information-Real Estate
Recording ----------------297-2641
Public Trustee ----------------297-2628
Releases-Public Trustee --------297-5179
C S U EXTENSION SERVICE
Ext Agent Lawn & Garden Home
Economics 4-H & Nutrition
1300 E Virginia Av --------297-2716
COMMISSION ON COMMUNITY
RELATIONS

ADAMS COUNTY GOVERNMENT
COUNTY ATTORNEY
4 Av & Bridge Britn
COURTS----See U   Justice
Colorado
State Government Revenue Dept
EXTENSION OFFICE--------659-4150
E124 Av & Henderson Rd Britn
DEPARTMENT
659-2120

Salt Lake City, Utah shows reference to "University" listing

Utah State University
Agricultural Experiment Sta
1817 N Main Frmngtn--‡867-2490
Utah State University Extension Center
444 S 300 W ----------------328-5745
Agricultural Agents --------328-5745
Consumer Information Specialist ---328-5745
Cooperative Extension Service -----328-5745
Expanded Food & Nutrition Program-328-5745
Four-H Clubs ----------------328-5745
Home Economists -------------328-4184
Home & Garden Information ----328-5745
Weed Supervisor --------------521-7300
Utah Stor Transfer Agcy Kearns Bldg
Utah Su Bid Service
Agraz Jess 678 13 Av
446S Agren Arlen 1256 Oros Av ----364-3333
Agren R Ellen 1810 S Main --------266-5172
Agricultural Extension Service----485-8994
See Utah State University Extension Center
Agriculture Dept Info----
See Utah State University Extension Center
Agriculture Fur Breeders Co-Op----
See Utah State Government
Agriculture Fur Breeders Agricultu
Agua

ARAPAHOE COUNTY GOVERNMENT
ACCOUNTING 5606 S Court Pl
AGRICULTURE EXTENSION OFC----794-9211
2379 W Main
4-H Club Agent 2379 W Main --------798-8533
Extension Home Agent
2379 W Main --------798-8533
AIRPORT 7625 S Peoria --------798-8533
5606 S Court Pl --------771-075

JEFFERSON COUNTY GOVERNMENT
RT HOUSE 1700 Arap Gln --------279-6511
LL OF JUSTICE
15200 W 6 Av Gln-279-5575
Traffic Engineer 701 Wier Gln---279-5527
EXTENSION OFC
15200 W 6 Av Gln --------279-4511
4-H Club 15200 W 6 Av Gln --------279-4511
FAIRGROUNDS & RECREATION
15200 W 6 Av Gln --------279-4391
After hours call--------279-4860
HEALTH DEPARTMENT --------238-630
260 S Kpling
INDUSTRIAL DEVELOPMENT

State Extension Service offices

AZ: Coop. Ext. Svc., *Univ. of Arizona*, Tucson AZ 85721.

CA: Public Service, University Hall, *Univ. of California*, Berkeley CA 94720.

CO: Bulletin Rm., *Colorado State Univ.*, Fort Collins CO 80521.

ID: Mailing Rm., Agricultural Science Bldg., *Univ. of Idaho*, Moscow ID 83843.

MT: Extension Mailing Rm., *Montana State Univ.*, Bozeman MT 59715.

NV: Agricultural Communications, *Univ. of Nevada*, Reno NV 89507.

NM: Bulletin Office, Dept. of Agricultural Info., Drawer 3A1, *New Mexico State Univ.*, Las Cruces NM 88001.

OR: Bulletin Mailing Service, Industrial Bldg., *Oregon State Univ.*, Corvallis OR 97331.

UT: Ext. Publications Officer, Library 124, *Utah State Univ.*, Logan UT 84321.

WA: Coop. Ext., Publications Bldg., *Washington State Univ.*, Pullman WA 99163.

WY: Bulletin Rm., Col. of Agriculture, *Univ. of Wyoming*, Box 3354, Univ. Station, Laramie WY 82070.

Why prune...?

Better have a reason for it

- Prune to direct growth . . .
- Prune to renew growth . . .
- Prune to produce more flowers . . .
  But don't prune blindly.
  Don't prune just because
  "It's the thing to do."

First let's take a look at the power you have in your fingertips to direct the pattern of growth of shrubs and trees.

The energy in a plant constantly flows to terminal buds throughout the plant. By pinching out terminal buds you can direct the growth of the plant. Pinch out buds on the right side of the plant and, until new terminal buds are formed, energy flows to the left side and to the top.

Pinch or prune tips of lower branches of a young tree and you speed up top growth.

To be a successful director of growth requires some study of the growth of plants and some experimental pruning. Every plant has its own particular way of growing. The reaction to pruning differs between kinds of plants. In some cases, pinching out a tip is followed by a quick growth of buds just below the cut; in other plants tip pinching is followed by growth of many lateral twigs all along the tipped branch.

It's a good idea—and a part of the adventure of gardening—to test the reaction to pruning by making a minor cut or two before you attempt to redesign the structure of a shrub or tree.

Direct growth in other ways

You direct growth in another way. When cutting back a stem to a bud, the position of the bud determines the direction of new growth. If the bud is on the right side the new branch will grow to the right. You can make a shrub more open or more dense by the selection of position of buds below the cut.

You direct growth again when you nip out the tips or first top bud of many annuals and perennials. You control the branching of chrysanthemums by repeated cutting back. To make these annuals bushy: tip out sweet peas when 5 inches high; snapdragons when they have only 4 or 5 sets of leaves; marigolds and zinnias when the first flower bud is formed. And you direct growth again when you remove faded flowers. Annuals direct their energy to seed production. Stop seed production and you prolong the flowering season.

Petunias respond beautifully to pinching out fading flowers. In removing old flowers, be sure to pinch below the seed case; just pulling out the blossom does no good.

When you plant annuals and perennials— zinnias, petunias, marigolds, marguerites, geraniums, etc.—pinch out tips (terminal buds) for full, many-branched plants.

Pruning for renewal

When pruning deciduous shrubs and trees you are working with this factor of plant growth: When a portion of a dormant plant is removed, the remaining parts of the plant will receive a larger share of the food stored in the roots, trunk, and limbs; larger share, that is, than they would receive if the plant were left alone.

You don't stimulate root growth by pruning out top growth. The new growth in spring is supported by food manufactured in the previous summer. In late summer and fall, large amounts of the food manufactured by the leaves is stored in roots, trunk, and limbs.

The language of pruning

In reading garden literature you will bump into a number of words and terms that have specific meanings to the experienced pruner. A full understanding of a few of these terms is a lesson in the laws of pruning as well as an aid in understanding pruning directions.

THIN OR THINNING OUT. To remove small or large branches back to side branch or main trunk. You make fewer cuts, leave fewer stubs, and maintain a more natural look when you thin rather than head back.

HEADING BACK. Cutting a branch back to a bud or side branch. This operation generally increases the bushiness of a plant, while thinning opens up the plant. The natural look of shrub or tree can be maintained if cuts are made with the natural shape of the plant in mind. Too often plants are whacked back.

NEW WOOD. New stem growth during one season.

before

thinning   *heading back*

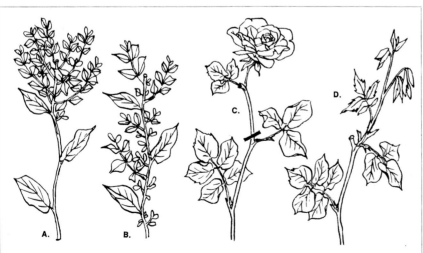

Here are 2 responses to tip-pinching—a quick growth of buds just below the cut (A) and the growth of many laterals all along the tipped branch (B) In other plants, like the rose shown here, a cut just above a bud (C), activates that bud and produces a vigorous new branch (D).

OLD WOOD. Growth of previous seasons. Often referred to by number of seasons—1-,2-, 3-year-old wood.

NODE. A joint in the stem. The point where a leaf starts to grow. General rule is to make cuts just above a node or bud.

Deciduous flowering shrubs

Many deciduous shrubs are pruned for gradual renewal by thinning out old wood. Every year or two you take out a few of the oldest canes at ground level. Removing old wood opens the top to let light and air into the interior of the shrub and encourages growth from the base that will eventually renew the top. Here are a few examples:

FORSYTHIA. Cut all 4-year-old to the ground. If long shoots with few buds develop in summer, pinch them back.

MOCKORANGE. It blooms best on 2 and 3-year-old wood.

BEAUTY BUSH (Kolkwitzia), *weigela,* and *pearl bush* (Exochorda) are thinned out every 2 or 3 years.

Flowering shrubs with a mound-like habit of growth should be pruned yearly by thinning out some of the weakest canes and cutting the remainder back to varying heights so the flowers will not all be on the same level. Shrubs in this class are the summer-flowering spirea, snowhill hydrangea, vitex.

Summer-flowering shrubs are pruned in the dormant season. Their flowers are borne on new wood developed in the spring.

The usual advice for pruning spring-flowering shrubs is "prune immediately after flowering." If you miss the very short pruning time following flowering, don't worry. You can prune in the dormant season without losing too many flowers. There will be enough old weak wood (with just a few flowers) to allow you to thin the plant without reducing spring flowering to any extent.

Hedges

PRIVET. To get a hedge of solid green, set plants close together and immediately cut back to 6 inches. This cutting makes sure that the hedge will be dense and green from the ground up. At the end of the first growing season, cut back again to 12 inches or lower. During the second summer cut back top growth half way several times.

To keep a full grown hedge dense, trim frequently during summer. Don't let the top become wider than the base. When a hedge is wider at

To make a pine more dense, wait for newly formed candles in the spring.

When these candles reach about 2 inches in length cut back halfway. This will induce new growth of buds in the whorls and a bushier plant.

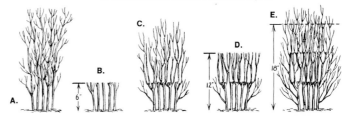

STARTING A PRIVET HEDGE RIGHT

Set the plants (A) Immediately cut them down to 6 inches (B) Allow the hedge to grow the first season with no summer pruning (C) At the end of the first growing season, cut back to 12 inches (D) Growth during the second season may be cut back to 18 inches during the summer (E).

top, the top casts a shadow on the base, causing death to the lowest branches and a bare-legged hedge.

Conifers to selectively prune

FIRS AND SPRUCE. In early spring cut back individual twigs to where side buds have formed in fall and winter. Or cut back new shoots when they are about half formed in June.

PINES. To make pines more dense, cut back newly formed candles about half when they reach about 2 inches in length (A). New buds will form at the base of the cut candles (B).

Broad-leaved evergreens

If pruning is needed to keep plants in scale for landscaping effects, do it in spring just before new growth starts. Prune to retain natural form of plants. Selective thinning and heading back will do it.

When using either a hook-and-blade or blade-and-anvil pruning shears, be sure the blade is on the bottom to prevent splitting and tearing the bark.

With loppers, too, you get a cleaner cut if the hook is on top. At a crotch where the hook won't fit, cut from the side with the blade next to the main branch.

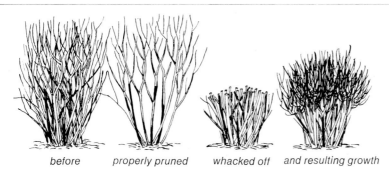

before properly pruned whacked off and resulting growth

A well pruned shrub retains its natural shape and habit of growth. Remove some of the old mature stems and any dead, diseased, or damaged canes right down to the ground. Just whacking off the top of a shrub often causes top-heavy bushiness that destroys the plant's natural shape and beauty.

Some kids have a way of riding through the stumbling blocks

A three or four feet tall gardener seems to be able to go right ahead and ride through stumbling blocks that might discourage the most ardent adult gardener. It's not just size, although it may be easier to look a bug in the eye when you don't have to bend down so far. It seems to be a combination of things, among which is a free-wheeling curiosity.

The Blake garden was an adventure garden. We hoped that some of the wonders of plant growth would catch the children's attention, quicken their curiosity. Teaching them how to grow vegetables was incidental to inviting them to see the natural world around them.

The structuring in the garden-raised beds, bean tunnels, teepees, and fence garden gave the garden interest even before the vegetables gave it form. The photographs tell the story.

Our years of experience with the Children's Adventure Garden in the University of California's Blake Garden, and three years with Mary Landis and her pre-school and kindergarten kids, have given us a profound respect for the interests and achievements of young gardeners. To some children, plants are really things to care for, love and play with. They nourish them with a certain amount of benign neglect and tenderness that creates wonders!

AT THE BLAKE-CHILDREN'S ADVENTURE GARDEN, experimentation—doing it your own way, was the basic idea. The children learned about gardening as they played around it. They rode over obstacles because no obstacles were made visible. Carol Malcolm, landscape architect student talks of her experiences with a group of children, ages 4 through 10, that visited the garden the first year of its operation:

"The children had the option to plant a great variety of seeds. If the results several weeks later were disappointing, they now had the option to take anything out, replant, or leave it alone.

"The children began to see the effects of their various planting and maintenance practices—often the seed had been washed away, planted too hastily, or inadvertently dug up.

"They felt the natural impact of animal (mostly deer) and human traffic, and began suggesting preventative measures. Some of the results were unexpected and pleasing: the grazed-off lettuce leafed out again, the second crop of peas grew more vigorously, and the lettuce planted in a main path matured in spite of all odds!

"The results of the somewhat random approach were very interesting. In an otherwise bare plot, a strange plant emerged that we later realized was a vegetable spaghetti. In another, the stubby gourd that seemed to have stopped growing suddenly shot up and sent out exotically white and crinkly blossoms. 'What's this weird flower going to be?' asked one 7 year old, pointing to her lettuce which had bolted in her absence. She was quite satisfied to leave it growing among her marigolds and zinnias.

"One mother who had three children involved in the garden noted their responses by age:

Paul, 4, wanted very much to work constructively; he became an avid waterer and loved the excitement of putting seed in the ground. He was a keen observer of detail—the kind you find 3 feet above the ground. The huge, velvety leaf of a Sparmannia, the mottled beans of the scarlet runners were wonderful treasures, and he was the first to notice the ripening tomato on the bush.

Diane, age 7, was more concerned with the visible aspects of growth in her own garden. Working in her own plot was very important to her and its apparent success or failure was a great concern. ('Why aren't my cucumbers growing like Christy's?') At the same time being with her friends was almost equally important.

Ross, age 10, was more experimental in his approach. At first he and a friend planted unusual vegetables in unconventional places, like in the pathway outside his plot. If his first attempts failed, he immersed himself easily in new ones. He worked carefully and thoroughly on his garden and even nursed a crookneck squash, which he had transplanted in bloom, into new growth. He also was quite helpful in explaining things to the younger children and was probably the most observant of the garden's overall development.

If you, like Ross, are a plant enthusiast and want to experiment, go ahead. Be a child again. Since children have very few rules and follow their own interests and ways of doing things, there can be unexpected results, and rewards.

THE MARY LANDIS YEARS were quite different. The involvement with the kids was in the classroom, rather than in part of a large garden. With Mary, there was the school system, and teaching methods to consider. What help should we ask for? Should we ask 4-H for help? What would a teacher need to know to expose her children to the green world? We answered some of these questions in a book called A Child's Garden. This book, now expanded to 52 pages, is published by the Public Relations Department of the Chevron Chemical Company, 200 Bush St., San Francisco, CA 94120. It is available at no cost to teachers and 50¢ to non-teachers.

A condensation of 5 pages in the book appears in the right hand column. Although fully aware that plants can't think, feel, be sad or happy, the plant called "Joey" plays an important role in the book. Joey talks about the principle of plant growth, and leaves all of the special recipes and false stumbling blocks for the adults. As Joey says . . . "Some like it hot; some like it cool; some like it wet; and some like it on the dry side. Here's some seeds. Let's find out."

A plant called Joey

A short course in plant physiology for teacher or parent, Joey was used to give the kids the basic principles of gardening.

Roots require a flow of air (oxygen) into the soil and a flow of their respiration product (mostly carbon dioxide) out of the soil. Compacted soil resists air flow, making it difficult for many plants to thrive.

Most growing failures can be traced to bad water management. Too much water in the soil drives out air and shuts off the oxygen supply causing root damage or death.

Leaves are food factories. They require mineral nutrients in a water solution. But, too much at one time can kill a plant.

Some plants tolerate shade and suffer in high light intensities. Most plants, when placed where there's too little light, become weak and thin.

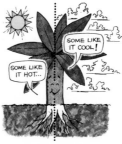

Different plant groups have different temperature requirements. There are warm-season plants and cool-season plants. (See planting chart, pages 88-89.)

In nature all plants are continually competing with each other for the available supplies of water, light, nutrients and the space in which to grow.

Some insects injure plant tissue, remove plant juices, inject toxins and transmit viruses. And many parasites —fungi and bacteria—attack leaves, stems.

Physical injury to roots, stems, branches or leaves may be caused by transplanting or cultivation. Also. by animals and small boys.

Saturday was the official day of the plant sale. We held a special preview sale on Friday for the parents and children who could not make it on Saturday. Friday we organized the tables and took apart the Plant Book and hung the pages which pictured each variety on the table

Stumbling blocks seem to be for adults only

The Mary Landis kinder-gardeners grew flowers and vegetables from seed to market-sized transplants and then staged a successful plant sale. Let that be a lesson to all of us who worry about our lack of expertise in gardening.

We asked Mary to look backward over the year and pick out some of the highlights that led up to the sale. Here are her words: "From the beginning, I have felt that the holidays with any plant association were naturals for child involvement. There was bound to be family talk about the holidays. The children could understand the good sense of preparing for them.

"Halloween and Thanksgiving were easy—pumpkins, of course, and then corn. Easter—anything growing in an eggshell. For St. Valentine's Day

we decided to force tulips into early bloom. There was a choice of flowers for Mother's Day, preceeded by many weeks of learning about seeds, and growing seedlings into flowering plants to take home.

"At the beginning of the year, the room had a root view box, a gro-light, and not enough window sills! By the time of the Plant Sale we looked like a full fledged junior nursery.

Tulips for St. Valentine's day

"Planting tulip bulbs for Valentine's Day took place in late November. We dissected bulbs and talked about what they need to grow. I drew a chart of the stages of growth of a tulip.

"The kids were fascinated with the chart: 'This is the first stage, now see the shoots shooting up. It's growing now!'

"We planted the bulbs in milk cartons and set them outside in a dark shed. When we returned from Christmas vacation, each bulb had new growth above the carton and roots oozing out the bottom. The kids said: 'Look at the roots!' 'He's choking in there.' So we transplanted into larger milk cartons cut in half.

"The tulips bloomed ahead of schedule. We had brought them inside too soon. But, we kept them going until the children took them home.

Growing bouquets for Mother's Day

"For Mother's Day we grew 'Wee Willie' Dianthus (dwarf Sweet William) and 'Tiny Tim' Alyssum with great success. The children loved these variety names.

"The kids seemed to go all out on the projects. In fact, they started some of their own! Chris and Andy just couldn't wait to plant outside. They planted germinated bean seeds against the play yard fence. It was a week before I was informed. They were pale and spindly because of cold weather and lack of sun, but they made it long enough to blossom! That was the glory!

The plant sale

"Our decision to have a plant sale came a little late, but it gave some new dimensions to the year's gardening activities. The kinds of plants to be grown, the best pots or cartons

holding that variety of plant. There were three children at each table to sell the plants and a parent "in the wings" to assist if necessary. The time was broken into one hour shifts. There was a different group of children and parents to help with the sale for each shift.

to grow them in and amount of money to charge for each were important topics for discussion.

"We really went on a plant growing spree with the Plant Sale as the object. Kys Cubes, Jiffy Pots, and Peat Pots were used to grow from seed to transplant size. The amazing transition of the Jiffy Pot in expanding to full size when put in water brought lots of excited discussion: 'Was it ever squished together!' 'Wow!' 'Look at the little pot poof!'

"Into the various cubes and pots we grew peppers, squash, pumpkins, cucumbers, tomatoes, basil, dwarf and tall marigolds, dahlias, and balsam. With each variety of flower or vegetable planted, I showed lots of pictures and discussed what the plant needed to survive. Taking the plants one at a time we talked of needs for sun, water, and when to plant to be ready for the Plant Sale.

"We made an illustrated Plant Book for our library about the plants we were growing. It helped others to share our experiences and turned out to be good reinforcement for everyone.

"There simply wasn't enough space for all of the plants in our classroom.

Another kindergarten and a second grade were invited to share our activities.

"Since the plants were grown indoors with artificial light and very weak window light, they needed to be 'hardened' to the outside world. So, the children on arriving at school in the morning would carry the flats of plants outside to the filtered shade of an oak tree in the play yard.

"Money was an important topic for discussion in planning the sale. The children valued the plants highly. 'This plant's worth $5 . . . well . . . maybe $4.' It took a while for the prices to come down.

At the plant sale

"The children took turns taking money and making change (with a little adult assistance in the background). One customer with a boxful of plants handed Victor a twenty dollar bill to pay for her three dollar purchase. Victor smiled, put the twenty dollar bill in the cigar box and said 'Thank you!' He was helped with a quick lesson in change making arithmetic!

"The kids wanted their plants to be

appreciated by the buyers. Thor and John were in charge of the 'Special Deal' table. Concerned about the pepper plants that were in Jiffy 7's, they were instructing each customer not to poke the tag in the pot, 'because it's full of roots and you'll hurt the plant.' They showed the buyers how to carry the plants and gave directions for their proper care.

"It was hard to part with the plants. Some of the children bought their own plants with their own money. Others talked parents and friends into buying 'just one more, 'cause they're so beautiful.'

"And, there were some shared sorrows. Sherry and Randy came in the week after the sale and reported their mothers had 'killed' the plants they bought. Sherry said, 'Mom broke the stem. You know what that means. The water couldn't get to the leaves and they turned brown and died.' Randy told us his mother put the plants outside while they were still too tender, and 'they burned.'

"We all agreed our sale was a hit! Financially it grossed enough to fund more gardening projects next year, pay our debts, and have an all-out celebration 'just for fun.' "

How to use the planting chart

"Depth to plant seed." A quick look at the fractions and you know that many gardeners plant too deep.

"Number of seed to sow per foot." It's one answer to the question "How thick or thin should I sow seeds?" Our figures give the average of 6 expert seed-sowers—3 pessimists and 3 optimists.

"Distance between plants." First figure is minimum. You get better growth at wider spacing. You cut down on the competition.

"Distance between rows." The minimum distance assumes that space is limited and weeding will be done by hand tools. Wider distance between rows is preferable and if power equipment is used, necessary.

"Number of days to germination." Number of days varies by soil temperature. Early spring sowings will take longer than later plantings. We give the range to answer questions like this one: "How long do I wait before I know I have to reseed?"

"Soil temperatures for seed." Seeds that "require cool soil" do best in a temperature range of 50°-65°; that

"tolerate cool soil" in a 50°-85° range; those that "require warm soil in a 65°-85° range.

"Weeks needed to grow to transplant size." The variation of 4-6, 5-7, 10-12 weeks allows for hot-bed, greenhouse, and window sill, and under grow-lamp conditions. Generally the warmer the growing conditions the shorter the time to grow transplants.

"Days to maturity." Figures in this column show the *relative* length of time needed to grow a crop from seed or transplant to table use. The time will vary by variety and season.

Vegetable	Depth to plant seed (inches)	Number of seed to sow per foot	Distance between plants (inches)	Distance between rows (inches)	Number of days to germination	Soil temperature for seed			Weeks needed to grow to transplant size	Days to maturity	Remarks
						Needs cool soil	Tolerates cool soil	Needs warm soil			
Artichoke	½		60	72	7-14		•		4-6	1 year	Start with divisions preferred.
Asparagus	1½		18	36	7-21		•		1 year	3 years	Sow in spring and transplant the following spring.
Beans: Snap Bush	1½-2	6-8	2-3	18-30	6-14			•		45-65	Make sequence plantings.
Snap Pole	1½-2	4-6	4-6	36-48	6-14			•		60-70	Long bearing season if kept picked.
Lima Bush	1½-2	5-8	3-6	24-30	7-12		•	•		60-80	Needs warmer soil than snap beans.
Lima Pole	1½-2	4-5	6-10	30-36	7-12			•		85-90	
Fava—Broadbean Winsor Bean	2½	5-8	3-4	18-24	7-14		•			80-90	Hardier than the common bean.
Garbanzo—Chick Pea	1½-2	5-8	3-4	24-30	6-12			•		105	
Scarlet Runner	1½-2	4-6	4-6	36-48	6-14			•		60-70	Will grow in cooler summers than common beans.
Soybean	1½-2	6-8	2-3	24-30	6-14			•		55-85 95-100	Choose varieties to fit your climate. See text.
Beets	½-1	10-15	2	12-18	7-10		•			55-65	Thin out extra plants and use for greens.
Black-eye Cowpea Southern Peas	½-1	5-8	3-4	24-30	7-10			•		65-80	
Yardlong Bean Asparagus Bean	½-1	2-4	12-24	24-36	6-13			•		65-80	Variety of Black eye peas. Grow as pole bean.
Broccoli, sprouting	½	10-15	14-18	24-30	3-10		•		5-7*	60-80T	80-100 days from seed.
Brussels Sprouts	½	10-15	12-18	24-30	3-10		•		4-6*	80-90T	100-110 days from seed.
Cabbage	½	8-10	12-20	24-30	4-10		•		5-7*	65-95T	Use thinnings for transplants. 90-150 days from seed.
Cabbage, Chinese	½	8-16	10-12	18-24	4-10		•		4-6	80-90	Best as seeded fall crop.
Cardoon	½	4-6	18	36	8-14		•		8	120-150	Transplanting to harvest about 90 days.
Carrot	¼	15-20	1-2	14-24	10-17		•			60-80	Start using when ½" in diameter to thin stand.
Cauliflower	½	8-10	18	30-36	4-10		•		5-7*	55-65T	70-120 days from seed.
Celeriac	⅛	8-12	8	24-30	9-21	•			10-12*	90-120T	Keep seeds moist.
Celery	⅛	8-12	8	24-30	9-21	•			10-12*	90-120T	Keep seeds moist.
Celtuce—Asparagus Lettuce	½	8-10	12	18	4-10		•		4-6	80	Same culture as lettuce.
Chard, Swiss	1	6-10	4-8	18-24	7-10		•			55-65	Use thinnings for early greens.
Chicory—Witloof (Belgian Endive)	¼	8-10	4-8	18-24	5-12		•			90-120	Force mature root for Belgian Endive.
Chives	½	8-10	8	10-16	8-12		•			80-90	Also propagate by division of clumps.
Collards	¼	10-12	10-15	24-30	4-10		•		4-6*	65-85T	Direct seed for a fall crop.
Corn, Sweet	2	4-6	10-14	30-36	6-10			•		60-90	Make successive plantings.
Corn Salad	½	8-10	4-6	12-16	7-10		•			45-55	Tolerant of cold weather.
Cress, Garden	¼	10-12	2-3	12-16	4-10		•			25-45	Seeds sensitive to light.
Cucumber	1	3-5	12	48-72	6-10			•	4	55-65	See text about training.
Dandelion	½	6-10	8-10	12-16	7-14		•			70-90	
Eggplant	¼-½	8-12	18	36	7-14			•	6-9*	75-95T	

*Transplants preferred over seed.

T Number of days from setting out transplants; all others are from seeding.

Vegetable	Depth to plant seed (inches)	Number of seed to sow per foot	Distance between plants (inches)	Distance between rows (inches)	Number of days to germination	Soil temperature for seed — Needs cool soil	Tolerates cool soil	Needs warm soil	Weeks needed to grow to transplant size	Days to maturity	Remarks
Endive	½	4-6	9-12	12-24	5-9		•		4-6	60-90	Same culture as lettuce.
Wonder Berry Garden Huckleberry	½	8-12	24-36	24-36	5-15			•	5-10	60-80	
Fennel, Florence	½	8-12	6	18-24	6-17		•			120	Plant in fall in mild winter areas.
Garlic	1		2-4	12-18	6-10		•			90-sets	
Ground Cherry Husk Tomato	½	6	24	36	6-13			•	6*	90-100T	Treat same as tomatoes.
Horseradish	Div.		10-18	24			•			6-8 mth.	Use root division 2-8" long.
Jerusalem Artichoke	Tubers 4		15-24	30-60			•			100-105	
Kale	½	8-12	8-12	18-24	3-10		•		4-6	55-80	Direct seed for fall crop.
Kohlrabi	½	8-12	3-4	18-24	3-10		•		4-6	60-70	
Leeks	½-1	8-12	2-4	12-18	7-12				10-12	80-90T	130-150 days from seed.
Lettuce: Head	¼-½	4-8	12-14	18-24	4-10	•			3-5	55-80	Keep seed moist.
Leaf	¼-½	8-12	4-6	12-18	4-10	•			3-5	45-60	Keep seed moist.
Muskmelon	1	3-6	12	48-72	4-8			•	3-4	75-100	
Mustard	½	8-10	2-6	12-18	3-10		•			40-60	Use early to thin.
Nasturtium	½-1	4-8	4-10	18-36			•			50-60	
Okra	1	6-8	15-18	28-36	7-14			•		50-60	
Onion: sets	1-2		2-3	12-24		•				95-120	Green onions 50-60 days.
plants	2-3		2-3	12-24		•			8	95-120T	
seed	½	10-15	2-3	12-24	7-12	•				100-165	
Parsley	¼-½	10-15	3-6	12-20	14-28		•		8	85-90	
Parsnips	½	8-12	3-4	16-24	15-25		•			100-120	
Peas	2	6-7	2-3	18-30	6-15	•				65-85	
Peanut	1½	2-3	6-10	30				•		110-120	Requires warm growing season.
Peppers	¼	6-8	18-24	24-36	10-20			•	6-8	60-80T	
Potato	4	1	12	24-36	8-16		•			90-105	
Pumpkin	1-1½	2	30	72-120	6-10			•		70-110	Give them room.
Purslane	½	6-8	6	12	7-14			•			
Radish	½	14-16	1-2	6-12	3-10	•				20-50	Early spring or late fall weather.
Rhubarb	Crown		36	60			•				Matures 2nd season.
Rocket	¼	8-10	8-12	18-24	7-14		•				
Rutabaga	½	4-6	8-12	18-24	3-10		•			80-90	
Salsify	½	8-12	2-3	16-18			•			110-150	
Salsify, Black	½	8-12	2-3	16-18			•			110-150	
Shallot	Bulb—1		2-4	12-18			•			60-75	
Spinach	½	10-12	2-4	12-14	6-14	•				40-65	
Malabar	½	4-6	12	12	10		•			70	
New Zealand	1½	4-6	18	24	5-10		•			70-80	
Tampala	¼-½	6-10	4-6	24-30			•			21-42	Thin and use early while tender.
Squash (summer)	1	4-6	16-24	36-60	3-12			•		50-60	
Squash (winter)	1	1-2	24-48	72-120	6-10			•		85-120	
Sunflower	1	2-3	16-24	36-48	7-12			•		80-90	Space wide for large heads.
Sweet Potato	Plants		12-18	36-48				•		120	Propagate from cuttings.
Tomato	½		18-36	36-60	6-14			•	5-7	55-90T	Early var. 55-60. Mid 65-75, Late 80-100.
Turnip	½	14-16	1-3	15-18	3-10	•				45-60	Thin early for greens.
Watermelon	1		12-16	60	3-12			•		80-100	Ice-box size mature earlier.

*Transplants preferred over seed.
T Number of days from setting out transplants; all others are from seeding.

Planting dates are made of rubber

It's been our experience that the vegetable gardener begins to know how to make the most of the climate of his garden after a year or two of trial and error plantings and faithful record keeping. Here we give you a starting point.

You can get a general fix on your climate and establish a pattern for your planting this way: take a look at the chart opposite showing the normal time to plant in the April to October growing season in relation to last and first frost dates. The sequence is based on the premise that cool weather crops need cool weather to mature in and warm weather crops need warm weather; that it is sometimes easier to find a cool ripening period in the fall than in the spring; that in some climates the cool period is in the winter months.

The basic plan is to start the hardy cool weather crops so they will mature *before* hot weather; to plant the warm weather crops when the weather warms and take advantage of the cool days of fall by planting in late summer or early fall depending on the length of growing season. If cool and warm weather designation is new to you, see the vegetable chart on pages 86, 87.

Knowing the weather preference of each vegetable it should be easy to fit it into the growing season of your garden—those days between the last frost of spring and the first frost of fall. In the bar chart on the following page we show the length of the growing season for representative cities of the West. (your climate will be similar to one of them). When you analyze the bar chart you realize that the length-of-growing season is sometimes a poor clue to your climate in terms of vegetable production.

In what pattern are such growth factors as sunlight and temperatures delivered? Contrast Boise and Seattle or Boise and Eugene, Oregon. The long growing season of western Washington and Oregon won't deliver in the same way as the shorter season

of Boise. Note the percentage of sunshine of each area and the rainfall figure. In Boise the warm growing weather comes quickly after the last frost, while in Seattle the period from the last frost date to the warm growing weather is long and wet.

In analyzing any climate the percent of possible sunshine is one of the key factors. All fruit-producing vegetables —tomatoes, corn, melons—need sunshine and high total heat units to produce quality crops.

This same type of contrast is apparent between San Francisco and Los Angeles. The length of the growing season says the climates are identical; percent of sunlight and temperatures show the difference.

For many a home gardener in areas where the last and first frost dates measure the growing season these dates seem to be made of rubber. A 200 day growing season may be 220 one year and 160 the next. "Last frost dates" published by the weather bureau are "normal" or "mean" dates. It's a date half way between the earliest and latest frost date of the spring season. There's a 50% chance that it will come earlier or later.

Make the most of the swing of the seasons

This chart of seasonal planting dates was prepared for the growing seasons of Long Island, New York. In principle it applies to all areas where the last frost date in spring is in April and the first frost date of autumn in October. Planting for fall and winter crops extends the harvest.

Early Spring

Plant as soon as ground can be worked in spring
Broccoli plants • Cabbage plants • Endive
Kohlrabi • Lettuce • Onion sets • Parsley
Peas • Radishes • Spinach • Turnips

Mid-Spring

Plant these at time of the average last killing frost
Carrots • Cauliflower plants • Beets
Onion seeds • Parsnips • Swiss Chard
Plant two weeks later:
Beans • Corn • Potatoes, early
Tomato seeds

Early Summer

Plant when soil and weather are warm
Beans, Lima • Cantaloupe • Celery plants
Crenshaw melons • Cucumbers
Eggplant plants.• Pumpkins • Pepper plants
Potatoes for winter • Squash • Tomato plants
Watermelons

Mid-Summer-Fall

Plant in late June or early July
Beets • Broccoli • Cabbage • Cauliflower
Kohlrabi • Lettuce • Radishes
Spinach • Turnips

Growing Season Climate

STATION	Growing Season Days	July Max./Min. Temp.	% of Sunshine	Inches of Rain	Days of Rain	Comments	Max./Min. Temp.
Butte, Mont.	110	80/50	77	5″	30	Short Cool	35/13
Durango, Colo.	121	84/48	76	7″	24	Short Mild	44/14
Provo, Utah	124	89/55	80	4″	30	Short Mild	39/19
Casper, Wyo.	130	87/56	76	5″	30	Shirt Mild	37/18
Cheyenne, Wyo.	130	85/55	70	7″	41	Short Mild	42/17
Billings, Mont.	132	88/61	76	6″	35	Short Mild	39/18
Great Falls, Mont.	135	85/54	79	8″	39	Shirt Mild	36/19
Reno, Nevada	141	89/46	90	1″	13	High & Dry	47/16
Pocatello, Idaho	145	90/55	82	3″	27	Warm Dry	36/18
Colo Springs, Colo.	148	84/57	68	9″	42	High Plains	45/19
Logan, Utah	157	90/56	80	5″	33	Mild Dry	38/16
Denver, Colo.	165	88/57	68	8″	43	High Plains	45/18
Pueblo, Colo.	167	92/61	72	8″	39	High Plains	49/18
Boise, Idaho	171	91/59	89	3″	26	Warm Dry	39/25
Spokane, Wash.	175	86/55	82	5″	38	Mild Dry	36/24
Medford, Ore.	178	88/56	78	6″	32	Pear Country	43/31
Yakima, Wash.	179	89/53	86	2″	23	Mild Dry	40/23
Pendleton, Ore.	183	89/58	86	4″	27	Mild Dry	43/30
St. George, Utah	196	100/66	80	4″	22	Utah's "Dixie"	54/28
Albuquerque, N.M.	196	91/66	76	4″	38	Mild Dry	48/26
Slt Lke City, Utah	202	94/60	82	7″	40	Warm Dry	39/21
Eugene, Ore.	205	82/51	74	11″	37	Mild Moist	48/36
Roswell, N.M.	208	95/62	76	9″	34	Warm Dry	57/21
Kingman, Ariz.	212	93/57	80	5″	26	High Desert	57/32
Kennewick, Wash.	218	89/63	86	7″	45	Apple Country	44/32
Las Vegas, Nev.	245	104/75	84	2″	15	Dry Desert	57/34
Tucson, Ariz.	261	98/74	77	8″	36	Dry Desert	65/39
Riverside, Calif.	265	94/57	80	5″	20	Citrus Country	68/38
Redding, Calif.	278	100/68	95	12″	40	Warm Dry	55/39
Portland, Ore.	279	79/56	70	22″	100	Rose Country	46/36
Seattle, Wash.	281	76/54	62	24″	108	Cool Showery	46/36
Fresno, Calif.	303	100/63	97	9″	28	Warm Dry	56/38
Pasadena, Calif.	313	88/58	75	9″	30	Rose Country	67/42
Phoenix, Ariz.	317	105/75	84	6″	30	Dry Desert	66/37
S.L. Obispo, Calif.	320	77/52	70	10″	37	Mild Coastal	66/43
Sacramento, Calif.	321	93/57	96	12″	46	Warm Dry	55/38
Eureka, Calif.	335	60/52	51	32″	102	Cool Wet	55/43
L.A., Calif.	365	83/63	80	14″	39	Mild Coastal	68/48
San Diego, Calif.	365	77/63	67	10″	44	Mild Coastal	67/47
S.F. Calif. (Arprt)	365	72/54	68	19″	62	Cool Coastal	57/43

Month scale headers above data: JAN. FEB. MAR. APR. MAY JUNE JULY AUG. SEPT. OCT. NOV. DEC.

People, climate and plants

When you map the home towns of the members of some plant societies you get a rough picture of the adaptability of the plant and the gardeners' reaction to it.

A plant that gets its own "society" must have a special relationship to people. This relationship is generally due to the multiplicity of species and varieties to be found under such names as Primrose, Camellia, Rhododendron, Iris, Hosta and others.

There's a mystery about these plants that is never completely solved. There seems always to be a new discovery in the plant's infinite variations. They challenge the inquisitive and call for the pooling of experiences through a society.

Climate is, of course, the major factor in the distribution of plants but there are other factors. The interest that people have in a plant has much to do with its distribution. One enthusiastic hobbyist may influence dozens of gardeners to see the plants as he sees them.

When you consider the primrose in all of its sections, species and varieties the ideal climate is in the cool, moist section of western Washington, Oregon and northern California. As other areas approach these soil and climate requirements so spreads the primrose.

The American Rhododendron Society reminds us that "over a thousand species, varying in size from tiny creepers to towering trees, offer exceptional variety to the gardener."

The Camellia is cultivated in a variety of climates in the United States, accepting winter temperatures as low as 10° (the hardiest varieties) and summer heat in the 100° range.

Joining a society is a way to greater enjoyment with plants and people.

American Primrose Society
Treasurer: Mrs. Lawrence G. Tait, 14015 84th Ave. N.E., Bothell, WA 98011. Dues: $5. Send for: "Pictorial Dictionary," $3 ppd.

American Rhododendron Society
Secretary: Bernice J. Lamb, 2232 N.E. 78th Ave., Portland, OR 79213. Annual dues: $10. Send for: "The Fundamentals of Rhododendron and Azalea Culture," 50¢.

American Camellia Society
Box 212, Fort Valley, GA 31030. Dues: $7.50. Send for: "Camellias for Beginners," $1.15 ppd.

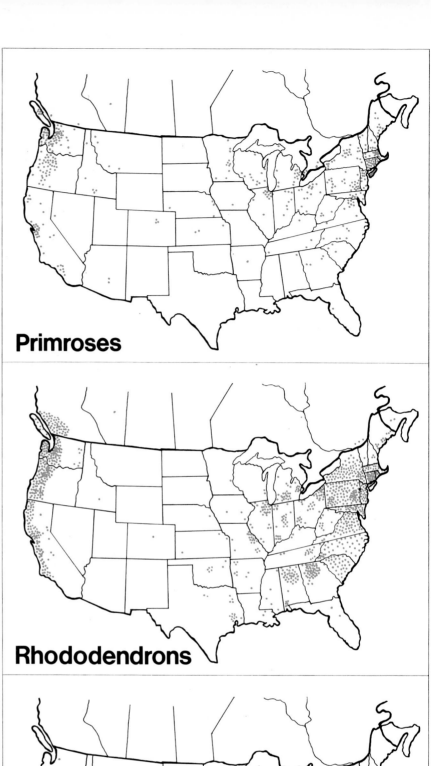

Primroses

Rhododendrons

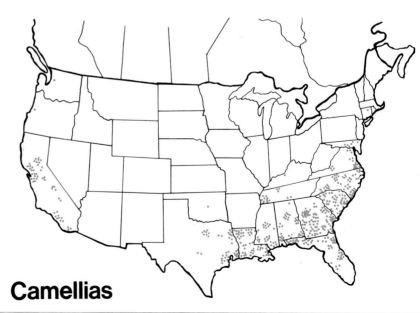

Camellias

Acid, Alkaline or Neutral Soil Reaction. Indicated by means of a pH scale. Soils below pH is between 5.8 and 7.2. To estimate pH, soil testing kits are available in many seed catalogs, nurseries and garden centers. For more accurate information, arrange for a soil test through your local county extension agent. (In telephone directory under State Government, Dept. of Agriculture).

A rule of thumb: High rainfall areas tend to have acid soil and light rainfall areas to have alkaline soil.

Agricultural lime is useful for correcting a very acid soil condition. In general a light application at regular intervals (about 5 lbs. of ground limestone per 100 sq. ft. every 5 years) maintains proper level.

Alkaline soils are reduced by the application of iron sulfate, aluminum sulfate or large amounts of sawdust, peat moss or ground bark.

Acre. A land area containing 43,560 square feet and measuring approximately 210x210 feet square.

Actual. That part of the formula for any product, containing several ingredients, which refers to a specific ingredient. For example, a 5-pound box of a general-purpose plant food 10-10-10 would have 10% nitrogen, 10% phosphate, and 10% potash. 10% of 5 lbs. is ½ pound. Therefore, the *actual* content of the three major ingredients in the mixture is ½ pound each.

Annual Plant. A plant living one year or less, usually planted in spring after the last frost and dying at time of killing frost. During this time the plant grows, blooms, produces seeds and dies (e.g. beans, sweet corn, cucumber, melon, marigolds, zinnias, sweet-alyssum).

Arboretum. An area devoted to the display of a variety of living trees and shrubs for study and comparison.

Auxin. A plant hormone that influences and regulates plant growth.

Ball (including Balled and Burlapped). Ball refers to soil encasing roots of plants being transplanted. The ball of soil around the roots, which keeps them from being disturbed, is often bound in burlap or similar mesh material. (Abbrev. B and B.)

Ball

Gardeners' Basic Terms

In the words of a friendly old timer—"Good old garden words got mixed up with new ones in the last few years.

My grandfather was (he had to be) an organic gardener when he buried salmon from the Columbia River, where the corn was to grow. My garden in Chehalis, Washington in 1920, grew without knowledge of *chelates, controlled release herbicides, ecology, environment, organic, vermiculite, perlite, peat pots, Fertl Pots, plastic mulch, metalized mulch, seed tapes, sodding, shredder-bagger, chipper, stress* or *bio-degradable.*"

"You can't put your foot in the same river twice. The 1920 river is very different from the 1975 river."

Here then, is a glossary of selected terms of the present and past used by gardeners from 20 to 75.

Bare Root. In the wintertime or in early spring, many varieties of deciduous plants are sold with their roots bare. Dormant plants, dug from the soil, have their roots cleaned and trimmed, and are prevented from drying out until the time they should be planted.

Bedding Plants. The term bedding plants refers to those plants sold in the nursery in flats or pony packs. They may be planted in beds, borders, or wherever it is desired.

Biennial Plants. A plant that completes its normal term of life in two years by flowering and fruiting in the second year.

Biodegradable. Any material that can readily be decomposed in the soil by the action of such micro-organisms as bacteria and fungi.

Bolting. The production of a seed stalk by vegetable plants such as spinach, lettuce or radish. Bolting by these crops in the garden is undesirable. Bolting usually occurs when days are long and temperatures are warm.

Bolting

Broadcasting. Scattering a material such as fertilizer or seed evenly over a soil surface.

Bulb

Bulb. A plant structure made up of a short, fleshy stem containing a growing point or flower bud. The stem is enclosed by thick, fleshy scales. (For other types see corm, rhizome, tuberous root).

Capillary Action. The attraction of soil particles to water molecules, causing an up or downward movement of the water into the soil. Becoming popular in container watering.

Catch Crop. A fast growing vegetable crop planted between rows of slow growing crops for best use of space. Also used during the period between harvest of early crops and sowing of late season crops as in *succession* planting or *intercropping*.

Chelate (ke'late). Several of the minor nutrients such as iron may be prevalent in the soil but unavailable to the plant because they're locked in, fixed into insoluble compounds that are unavailable to the plant. When a chelating agent with the micronutrient is added, the nutrient element is made available to the plant.

Chlorophyll. The green photosynthetic coloring matter found in plants, particularly in the leaves, where it is continually being manufactured. Known to have a vital role in converting carbon dioxide and water into simple sugars by the process of photosynthesis.

Chlorosis. Lack of green in a leaf, caused by nutritional failure or disease. It is most frequently caused by lack of a plant's ability to take up iron. In severe cases the entire leaf except the veins turns yellow. Often there is enough iron in the soil, but it's not available to the plant. Lowering the soil pH or using a chelate with iron will help correct most chlorotic conditions.

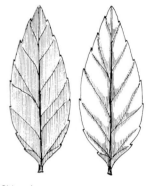

Chlorosis

Clone. A group of organisms derived from a single individual by asexual reproduction.

Clump. An aggregate of crowns or roots, able to be easily divided or moved.

Cluster. A bunching of flowers or leaves on a single stem. (The term is sometimes given to any grouping of twigs, leaves, fruits or flowers).

Cold Frame. A box which is not artificially heated but which protects plants from the elements. It is usually covered with plastic or cheese cloth or with a glass sash. Typical dimensions are: 4 ft. wide with a 12-in. front and an 18-in. back. Length is determined by the number of plants to be accommodated. It should be constructed so that it is moveable and can be placed in the sun or shade, depending on the season.

Cold Frame

Companion Crops. Crops which have different harvest dates but are grown in the same area at the same time. One crop is harvested and removed by the time the other crop requires the growing space.

Compost. A decomposing mixture of vegetable matter—leaves, grass clippings, weeds — which can be used as a fertilizer. Gardeners usually build a compost this way: first a 6- to 12-inch layer of vegetable matter, then an inch or so of soil. Decomposition is speeded up if a commercial fertilizer and lime are used. A practical way is to build up a six-inch layer of material, then cover with an inch of soil mixed with fertilizer and lime.

Conifer. Cone-bearing trees or shrubs, most often characterized by narrow, needle-like leaves. They are frequently referred to as evergreens. Examples: pine, cedar, juniper, cypress.

Conservatory. A glassed-in room or structure where temperatures and humidity are controlled, used for the growing of plants for display. (Unlike a greenhouse, a portion may be used for living purposes).

Contour Planting. Horizontal planting in rows that follow the contours of a slope or grade to better control water drainage and erosion of soil.

Contour Planting

Controlled Release. A descriptive term applied to fertilizers that release their nutrients in regulated amounts. These are (1) slightly soluble fertilizers that slowly dissolve in the soil, (2) plastic-coated fertilizers through which water slowly penetrates to release the soluble contents, (3) organically incorporated nutrients that are released by microbal breakdown.

Cool Crops. Vegetables which do not thrive in summer heat; e.g., the cabbage family, lettuce, spinach, peas.

Corm. A rounded, thick underground stem base, commonly called a bulb. However, a corm is unlike a true bulb in that food is stored in its center rather than in its scales.
Corm

Cover Crop. Sometimes referred to as "green manure," a cover crop is useful in large gardens where some of the soil lies dormant in winter. Any of the legumes (clover, cow peas, etc.)

sown in fall and turned under in early spring will return valuable humus and nitrogen to soil.

Creeper. Plants or vines growing close to the ground — properly speaking, plants that take root along their stems.

Crop Rotation. Practice employed by both gardeners and farmers for maintaining the good condition of a given section of soil by alternate planting of different crops. Such planting also helps to discourage insects which thrive on a given crop; or diseases indigenous to a certain kind of plant.

Cross Pollination. Accomplished by either insects or wind, the transfer of pollen from the anthers of one flower to the stigma of another in order to effect fertilization of an ovary; fertilization must take place before seed can be produced.

Crown. The part of the plant where the stem and root join.

Cultivar. A term meaning cultivated variety now used in place of the word variety to indicate a specific type of horticultural plant. Cultivars may differ in growth habit, season of maturity, fruit color, fruit shape, etc. Example-'Detroit Dark Red' beet. They are properly, but not always, set apart in single quotes.

Cultivation. The loosening of a soil with either a hand- or mechanical-type implement chiefly for the purpose of controlling weeds.

Culture. A specialized activity used in growing plants (e.g., pruning, cultivation, watering).

Cutting (or slip). A way to propagate plants by breaking or cutting off a portion of a branch or root and planting it in soil or water so that it can grow roots and in time become a plant exactly like the parent one.

Cutting Height. In mowing lawns, the measurement from grass clipped to soil line.

Damping Off. A plant disease owing to fungus in the soil. Causes seedlings to die immediately before or just after they break through the soil. Careful watering, good drainage and disinfecting seed bed soil help in preventing damping off.

Day-Neutral. A term applied to plants which are not affected by the relative length of dark and light periods.

Deciduous. A plant that sheds all its leaves at one time once a year.

Deep Rooted. Plants with deeply growing roots as contrasted with roots growing on or close to the surface.

Determinate Tomato. (Commonly called Bush tomato.) Terminal bud sets fruit, stops stem growth. The plant is self-topping. Seldom needs staking.

Dew. Condensed moisture from the atmosphere adhering in the form of small drops to any cool surface.

Dew Point. A temperature point below which moisture in the atmosphere is condensed into small drops.

Dibble or Dibber. A handheld pointed tool for making holes in the soil for planting seeds, bulbs, transplants, etc.

Dividing. A method for increasing plants such as bulbs and perennials and other plants that spread by developing roots and tops in clumps (e.g., dahlias, iris, daylilies). Accomplished by digging up all or a portion of a plant, breaking apart the rooted sections, and replanting.

Dormancy. Cyclic period when a plant rests and its growth processes greatly slow down. This occurs in many species by the coming of winter as days grow shorter and temperatures begin to drop. The period ends in spring when the plant is exposed to higher temperatures for an extended number of hours. Dormancy is a plant's safeguard against extremes of temperature, etc.

Dormant Oil. An oil emulsion in spray form which is used during a plant's dormant period to control scale and other insects.

Dormant Spray. An insecticide applied to a plant during the winter or in very early spring, usually before active plant growth begins, for the control of diseases and insects. Dormant oil and lime sulfur sprays are most often used for this purpose.

Drainage (Water). A term used to describe how water passes through root areas of plants. This passage is essential to the proper growth of almost all plants.

Drainage (Air). A term used to describe the circulation of air (oxygen) into the soil and the flow of respiration product (mostly carbon dioxide) out of the soil. Compacted soil around roots resists air flow, making it difficult for many plants to thrive. Also refers to movement of air from adjacent areas to effect temperature changes for sensitive growing crops like citrus.

Drill. A tiny furrow made with the corner of hoe or pointed stick, a bit deeper than the seed to be planted. All vegetables grown from seeds planted in straight rows are sown in drills.
Drill

Drip Irrigation. A system for watering at points on or just below the soil surface so that only small areas are moistened. The irrigation should be made with very low water pressure over a long period of time so as to supply plants with only the amount of moisture needed to replace the plants' moisture loss.

Drip Line. A line drawn around a tree directly under the outermost ends of its branches, the point at which rain water drips off. Term is used in connection with watering and fertilizing trees.
Drip Line

Dry-off. A method often used to help a plant or bulb enter dormancy or a rest period in good condition by gradually reducing the amount of water it normally receives.

Dust. Thoroughly blended mixture of a toxicant and filler, usually a clay. The toxicant is present in relatively small percentage and the filler serves as a carrier, much as water does in spray mixtures. A dust is quicker spray mixtures.

Dwarf. A plant which is undersized for its age, but is at the same time strong and healthy.

Early. A descriptive term applied to certain vegetables that mature faster than others of the same species; i.e., faster growing variety.

Easement. The right by law for one party to make limited use of land owned by another party.

Ecology. The study of living things in their environment and the inter-dependence between all forms of life and their natural habitats.

Environment. The complete surroundings of an organism or an ecological community.

Espalier. A plant (tree or shrub) trained to grow flat against a surface such as a wall or trellis.

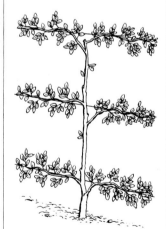
Espalier

Everblooming. Plants that bloom intermittently during the entire growing season.

Evergreen. A plant which does not lose all its leaves at one and the same time. See conifer.

Everlasting. Various plants or flowers that will not lose their color or shape when dried.

Exotic. Referring to plants that are introduced to a region other than that to which they are considered natives.

Extension Service. A function of the Federal, State and County Cooperative Extension system that provides agricultural and home economics information to residents of the states. Each state has a Land Grant University conducting research and providing educational publications. Most counties have an extension agent, and many have gardening information for distribution. For more details, see pages 78 & 79.

Fertilizer. A material which provides one or more mineral nutrients in forms which can be used by growing plants. The term generally refers to materials of organic or inorganic origin that are known to increase nitrogen, phosphate and potash when added to soil or dissolved in water.

Fibrous Root System

Fibrous Root System. Made up of many-branched roots and rootlets (sometimes with no taproot development) as distinguished from bulbous or tuberous roots.

Fill. Soil or other materials used to change the elevation or level the grade of an area.

Flat. A single shallow box or tray used to start cuttings or seedlings.

Flower. Usually a symmetrical form of colorful growth with the primary purpose being to produce seed for subsequent reproduction. The seed-bearing plant's reproductive organ.

Foliage Plant. Plants grown especially for the beauty of leaves or foliage as contrasted to those plants grown for flowers or fruit.

Foliar Feeding. The process of providing mineral nutrients to plant foliage and stems with soluble fertilizers.

Forcing. A method to speed up a plant's growth to maturity by growing it under a shelter, for instance glass, for increased heat.

Frond. The leaf of a palm tree or of a fern.

Frost. Temperature below the dew point, causing freezing condition and a covering of minute ice particles on exposed objects.

Fumigation. Applying chemicals or gases to control insects within an enclosed area or under a plastic cover.

Fungicide. A chemical material used to retard or prevent the growth of fungi.

Furrow. A small ditch (often V-shaped) made for deep seed planting or irrigating.

Fusarium Wilt. Wilting and yellowing of plant leaves caused by fungus disease which has attacked roots and most likely will kill plant.

G

Gazebo. An open garden structure or pavillion located on a site affording a pleasant view.

Genus. Describing the classification of a related family of plants consisting of one or more species.

Germination. The sprouting of a seed and the commencement of growth. (Also used to mean the starting of plants from seeds).

Grading. Modifying a ground area by cutting or filling to make it level.

Grafting. The process of implanting a scion (a detached living portion of a plant) into a growing plant (called the stock) so that cambium layers make contact with each other, thus allowing the scion to obtain nourishment (water and nutrients) from the stock. The end result is the union of the two plant parts.

Grain. Pertaining to lawns, describes the tendency of blades to lean in the direction of mowing or the grass to grow horizontally in certain directions other than vertically.

Green Manure. A cover crop which is turned under while still green. (See Cover Crop.)

Ground Cover. Refers to both plants and inert material, used to cover certain areas for the purpose of preventing soil erosion or to discourage the intrusion of undesirable plants. Also used as an ornamental in landscape design.

Growing Medium. Specially formulated soil substitute prepared for plant growing.

Growing Season. The period of time from the last plant-killing frost in the spring to the first plant-killing frost in the fall.

Growth Regulators. Any synthetic or natural organic compound such as indoleacetic acid, giberellin, abcisson, 2,4-D, napthalene acetic acid, etc., which in diluted amounts will promote, inhibit or modify plant growth processes; also called auxins, plant hormones and phytohormones. These hormones regulate leaf drop, root initiation, bud dormancy, bending of plants in response to light, etc.

H

Hardening. A process of slowing plant growth by withholding water, lowering the temperature, or gradually shifting the plants from a more sheltered environment to a less sheltered environment. The process of hardening plants is used to increase chances for survival at transplanting time.

Hardy Plant. A plant which can be planted before the last killing frost in the spring. The word hardy applied to plants means the ability to resist frost.

Heading Back. Pruning a branch back to bud or side branch in order to make the plant bushier.

Heaving. Occurs in winter as a result of alternate freezing and thawing. The soil cracks and lifts, often thrusting small plants out of the soil and damaging their roots. (May be at least partially counteracted by deep planting or by the application of a mulch).

Heavy Soil. A soil usually difficult to work. Clay soils are considered to be heavy soils.

Heeling In. A method for storing plants temporarily by burying or covering their roots with materials such as sawdust or soil.

Heeling In

Herbaceous Plant. A plant described as having a soft, non-woody stem. Generally, these plants live and grow for only one season.

Herbicide. Chemical used to destroy undesirable plants and vegetation.

Hills

Hills. In gardening terms, this means a group of three or four plants whose seeds, usually seven to ten in number, have been sown in a circle from twelve to fifteen inches in diameter, evenly spaced. After plants come up, all but three or four of the hardiest are removed from the soil.

Host Plant. Any plant that furnishes subsistence for a plant pest. In the literal sense, any plant that a bug or disease lives on is a host plant. In general usage, however, the term is used to describe a plant that is notorious for offering sustenance to any one bad pest—as cabbage family plants are host plants to harlequin plant bug; as wheat corn and native prairie grasses are hosts for chinch bugs in the South; and as barberries are hosts to blister rust.

Hotkap

Hotkap. A miniature hothouse which can be made in many ways (i.e. using top portion of plastic bottle or a wax paper cone) and used over seeds to force growth by providing additional heat as well as protection from frost, insects, birds, pets.

Humus. Decomposed organic matter producing a dark material in or on soil.

Husk. The dry outer covering of certain seeds, of which the most commonly known is the corn husk.

Hybrid. A plant resulting from crossing two plants of the same type which have different individual characteristics for a trait (e.g., tall or short for the height trait).

Hydroponics. The growing of plants in water (without any soil), to which nutrients have been added to provide for plant needs.

I

Impervious. Not penetrable by water or other fluids.

Indeterminate Tomato. The terminal bud does not set fruit. The vine can grow indefinitely if not killed by frost. Most of the varieties trained on stakes or in wire cages are in this group.

Indigenous. Plants native to a particular region. Opposite of exotic.

Insecticide. A material toxic to insects either by contact and/or stomach poisoning.

Interplanting. For the small garden a practical method for getting maximum production and variety by planting fast-growing varieties between slow-growing kinds. A good example is cauliflower planted between rows of corn about four weeks before the corn crop ripens.

Irrigation. Artificially applying water to the soil during periods when natural rainfall does not occur in enough volume to maintain a desirable level of soil moisture for plant growth.

K

Knot Garden. A planting design, similar to knots used in embroidery, incorporating ground covers, herbs, bedding plants, or low hedges. See photograph, page 70.

Lath. (House or screen). An overhead structure to protect plants from too much sunlight or from frost (e.g., spaced laths as a roofing).

Layering. A propagating technique in which the stem of a woody plant is bent down and buried in a rooting medium in order to force the development of roots along the buried portion of stem.

Layering

Leaching. Method for removing excess soluble salts or other impurities from topsoil by pouring water through the soil.

Leaf Mulcher. See shredder-bagger.

Leggy. A plant that is long and spindly, with sparse foliage at its base. The cause may be too much shade, overcrowding or overfeeding. This condition may be corrected if the plant is pinched back. (See Pinching Back.)

Legume. A plant whose root system is invaded by nitrifying bacteria. These bacteria may convert nitrogen into forms which can be utilized by the plant.

Lifting. Refers to the digging of a plant that is to be replanted.

Light Soil. A soil that is easy to work. Also a coarse textured soil such as sand.

Lime. Generally. the term lime is applied to ground limestone which is used as an amendment to reduce the acidity of acid soils. Dolomitic lime has magnesium carbonate and will supply some magnesium for the growing plant.

Loam Soil. A soil made up of equal parts of sand, silt and clay-sized soil particles. This composition provides a good soil texture suitable for plant growth.

Long Season Crop. A crop which requires a maximum of frost-free days to produce a satisfactory crop.

Macro. Prefix meaning large.

Manure. Organic material excreted from animals, used as fertilizer to enrich the soil.

Metalized Mulch. This is a film that is made with a silver or aluminum coating. This has the added advantage of increased light reflection, it also works as an aphid repellent, not readily available for the home gardener at the present time.

Micro. Prefix meaning small.

Micro-Climate. The climate of a small area or locality particularly near the ground level, as opposed to the climate of a county or state. e.g. A backyard or a portion of it.

Mildew. A white, cottony coating on plants which later turns them black and wrinkled. Caused by various fungi especially during periods of warm days and cool nights.

Mist. A procedure using vaporized water within an enclosed space to provide a constant moisture for plant growth when propagating.

Mulch. Any material applied to the soil surface to conserve soil moisture, maintain a more even soil temperature and/or aid in weed control. The mulch may be of manure, leaf mold, straw, sawdust or even paper.

Mutation. A change in a plant gene that produces a new variety differing from the parent.

Nematode. A minute, transparent, worm which decomposes organic matter. Some are parasites that infest roots, bulbs and leaves.

Nitrogen. Nitrogen is one of the most essential of all plant nutrients obtained from the soil. If the supply of nitrogen is good, foliage is green and the plant flourishes. Insufficient nitrogen is indicated by yellowing leaves and stunted growth. Too much nitrogen may cause excessive growth making plants more susceptible to frost and disease. A fertilizer that is rich in nitrogen can be added to the soil, or a crop (e.g. clover, cowpeas and other legumes) which absorbs nitrogen from the air and returns it to the soil can be sown. (See Fertilizer; NPK.)

Node. A joint or point where a branch, bud or leaf meets the stem from which it develops.

Nomenclature. The system of classification of botanical names as a result of international agreement. (See Taxonomy.)

NPK. The symbols for the big three nutrients needed by plants. N is for nitrogen; P is for phosphate; K is for potash. The percent of each element in a package or bottle of fertilizer is always shown in NPK order. Thus a 16-16-8 fertilizer is 16 per cent nitrogen, 16 per cent phosphate and 8 per cent potash. In addition to the above major elements, plants need calcium, magnesium and sulfur in relatively large amounts. Needed in trace amounts (minor elements) are: iron, manganese, boron, zinc, copper, chlorine and molybdenum.

Nutrient Solution. Liquid containing some or all of the mineral elements required for plant growth. Especially applied to use in hydroponics or water culture.

Organic Matter. A term applied to a substance containing carbon compounds and usually obtained from decomposed plants or animals. Needed to maintain a healthy soil structure and bacterial life. e.g. peat moss.

Ornamental. Refers to plants grown for beauty of form, flower or foliage rather than for food or fruit. However, many vegetables such as herbs, leeks and kale are considered equally ornamental as well as being edible.

Ortho. Prefix meaning straight, proper or correct.

Over-potting. Planting in pots larger than necessary for the root ball, causing the soil to become water saturated and poorly aerated.

Parasite. A pest or disease that lives on or within an organism of another species known as the host. The parasite obtains its nutrients from the host, leading to the deterioration or death of the latter.

Patented. Referring to cultivated plant varieties protected by government patent granting exclusive rights to patent holder.

Peat. Partially decayed organic plant matter from ancient swamps used for mulching and soil improvement.

Peat Pot. Made of compressed peat (or other like material), used for the starting of plants which are to be transplanted in the pot directly to the soil.

Perennial Plant. A plant which normally lives more than two years.

Perlite. A volcanic mineral expanded by heat treatment to form lightweight white granules. It is used either for soil conditioning or as a rooting medium for plants. Also, used in synthetic soil formulas, and as a substitute for sand in potting mixes.

Pesticide. A substance (most often a chemical) used to control weeds, fungi, insects and the like.

pH. The chemistry symbol used in expressing relative acidity or alkalinity.

Phosphate. Term for compounds of phosphorous, the second of 3 major plant nutrients listed in the fertilizer grade NPK. Required for plant growth. (See NPK.)

Photo Period. A term applied to hours of light required daily to achieve normal maturity. Plants are often referred to as long day plants, short day plants, or intermediate plants. The plants response to its photo period is known as photoperiodism.

Phototropism. The growth of plants toward light in response to light stimulus.

Pinching Back. A method for increasing side growth or making plants bushier by nipping off tips of branches with the thumb and forefinger.

Pinching Back

Pip. The small seed of the fleshy fruits such as apples, pears and citrus. Also an individual root stock having a single stem such as lily-of-the-valley.

Pit. The hard stone in fruit which contains the seed. Also a hole in the ground used to store plants needing protection during cold weather.

Plant Nutrient. One of the 16 chemical elements currently known as essential to plant growth.

Plant Spacing. The distance in inches or feet between individual plants growing in a row.

Plastic Mulch. One of the newer forms of mulching materials. Many polyethylene materials, sold under various trade names, are available either black or clear, slit or solid and in varying widths. Also see Metalized Mulch.

Pollen. Microscopic dust-like grains, produced on the anthers of flowers, which contain male sex cells. Dry pollen is transported by the wind, sticky pollen by birds and insects. Each pollen grain, after coming to rest on the stigma of a pistil, will produce sperm cells to fertilize an ovule.

Pollination. This term is used to mean the transfer of pollen from the stamens (staminate flower) to the pistils (pistillate flower). Plants are either cross-pollinating or self-pollinating. Cross pollinating means the transfer of pollen from flowers of one plant to the flowers of another (either of the same species or a different species). Self-pollinating takes place when pollen is transferred between the reproductive organs of an individual flower or between flowers on the same plant (e.g. sweet peas).

Pomology. The science of growing fruit.

Pot-Bound. A potted plant, the roots of which have become thickly matted, is said to be pot-bound. See Root-bound.

Pot-Bound

Post-emergence. Chemical treatment applied after the plants emerge from the soil level.

Potash. The third of three major plant nutrients listed in the fertilizer grade NPK. Essential for plant growth. Also refers to potassium carbonate, often obtained from wood ashes.

Potting. The transplant of any plant to a single pot.

Potting Mixture. A combination of various ingredients designed for growing plants in containers. Recipes or formulas are commonly circulated among good gardeners or you can buy potting mixtures pre-packaged wherever plants are sold.

Pre-emergence. Generally, chemical treatment of soil to kill weed seeds before they germinate or after a crop is planted but before it emerges.

Propagation. Reproduction of plants either from seeds (sexual reproduction) or from cuttings division, budding, grafting or layering (asexual reproduction).

Pruning. The wise removal of plant parts to obtain a more desirable plant.

Respiration. In popular language this term simply means "breathing." As applied to plants, it is the chemical process by which a plant absorbs oxygen, then releases energy from the oxidizing of plant sugars to water and carbon dioxide. Plant soil should be sufficiently aerated so that oxygen is able to get to the plant's roots.

Rest Period. A normal period in a plant's life when it does not grow any larger. Perennials, which have an annual cycle, grow to flower or fruit during part of a year, then rest during the remainder. Even plants in a temperate climate follow this pattern. (See dormancy).

Rhizome. An underground stem that spreads by creeping; produces shoots above and roots below.

Ripe. The stage at which growth has reached complete maturity for intended use, e.g. harvesting, eating.

Root-bound. Undesirable condition of a plant that has grown too long in a container so that its roots have become "choked."

Root Crop. The term used to describe crops grown for edible roots e.g. beets, carrots, turnips.

Root Cutting. A portion of a root or root stock used for propagation.

Root Pruning

Root Pruning. A method for fostering the development of a branched root system, helpful in transplanting or as a method of invigorating the plant.

Row. Generally speaking, planted by drill method (see under Drill). An exception is planting peas where seeds are scattered out.

Row Spacing. Distance in inches or feet between plant rows.

Runner. A long, thin, trailing stem that develops new plants when the nodes contact the soil. Strawberry runner is a typical example.

Rust. A fungus which infects garden plants such as roses. Characterized by round pustules filled with reddish or yellow spores on the leaves.

Scald. An injury to the bark of a woody plant, brought about by frost or by overexposure to sun, high temperatures or wind. Characterized by brownish spots on the bark. Also see Sun Scald.

Scale. In garden language this word has more than one meaning. It may mean a small oval insect with a shield-like covering, or a scale-like leaf which protects a leaf bud before it opens.

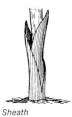

Scale

Scorch. A condition brought about by bacteria, drought, heat, over-use of insecticides, fungi or sun exposure, characterized by the yellowing or browning of a plant's foliage.

Screening. The use of plants to shut out an undesirable view.

Seed. The small grains produced by flowering plants containing embryos which germinate to produce new plants.

Seed Flats. Used for starting seeds, these are boxes, generally 3 to 4 inches deep; a popular size is 14 inches wide, 24 inches long.

Seed Germination. The beginning of growth of the young plant in a seed when heat moisture and air are provided.

Seed Starters. Known commercially as peat pots, Jiffy 7's, Kys Kubes & Fertl Cubes which are small growing units containing nutrients for seed germination. These can be transplanted directly into soil.

Seed Tapes. Seeds prespaced and enclosed into a water soluble plasticlike tape. When tape is planted, covered with soil and watered, tape dissolves.

Seedbed. The name given to a garden soil prepared to receive seeds or plants as a result of plowing and disking, tilling or spading and raking.

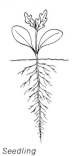

Seedling. The young plant emerging from a germinating seed. If seeds are sown thickly in a seed bed, for example, they soon begin to fight for sufficient growing room. As their true leaves appear, they should be transplanted to bed or box until they are ready for transplanting to the garden.

Seedling

Self-incompatible. Plants having flowers which must have pollen from other plants of the same species in order to become fertilized.

Self-pollination. (See Pollination).

Shade Tolerant. Plants which grow well in partial or even almost full shade (e.g. many perennials.) However, it should be remembered that most plants do best in areas receiving the sun for a number of hours per day or in filtered sunlight.

Sheath. A separate part of a plant, tubular in structure, which encases the lower end of a stalk.

Sheath

Short Season Crop. A crop which grows and produces its harvest within one or two months.

Shredder, Shredder-bagger, Shredder-grinder, Chipper. Machines designed to shred garden debris, branches, leaves, sod and so forth. Many also mix soil and concrete, and pulverize rock for decorative mulches.

Shrub. Generally smaller than a tree, a woody perennial which usually has numerous stems growing from its roots.

Side Dressing. Fertilizers applied close enough to a plant so that its root zone is provided with plant food. Commercial fertilizers should be scattered in a hollow trench parallel to a row, or in a circle around a hill, and thoroughly watered.

Side Dressing

Silt. A fine-grained type of soil sediment resulting from deposits of streams. When properly mixed with organic matter it makes an excellent garden soil.

Slip. A cutting pulled, broken or cut from a woody or herbaceous plant. (See Cutting.)

Small Fruits. As distinguished from tree fruits, these are fruits produced from vines or low-growing plants.

Sod. A surface of earth covered with grass. Also a section of ground containing top growth of grass and the matted roots used to cover bare soil.

Sodding. The process of covering a given area with turfgrass. Sods of turfgrass with adhering soil can be used in sizes varying from small plugs or strips to large blocks or squares.

Softwood Cutting. A cutting of a young shoot taken from a woody or herbaceous plant before it has hardened. These cuttings are then planted into a rooting medium for propagation.

Soil. The upper layer of the earth's surface, made up of organic material, minerals and miniscule living forms, in which plants grow.

Soil Aeration. The process of loosening or puncturing the soil by mechanical means in order to increase water and air permeability.

Soil Amendment. Used for such soil improvement as better drainage or moisture retention or aeration, by use of chemical or mineral added to the soil.

Soil-Borne Fungi. Small, non-green plants which live in the soil and are capable of causing plant disease.

Soil Crusting. The formation of a hard layer of soil on the soil surface.

Soil Improvement. Making soils more productive by such practices as adding organic matter, fertilizers and lime.

Soil Sterilization. Accomplished by fumigation, chemical, heat or steam, a process by which soil is made free of harmful organisms.

Soil Testing. A scientific analysis of a soil sample's acidity, texture and chemical composition in order to gauge the suitability of the soil for certain uses or to determine the modifications necessary to adapt it to a wished-for use.

Soil Texture. This means the size of the soil particles giving the proportion of clay, sand and silt in a given soil.

Soilless Culture. The practice of growing plants in a nutrient solution without the use of garden soil. (See Hydroponics.)

Species. A group of plants closely resembling each other and which interbreed freely.

Sphagnum. A group of mosses which grow in bogs. Peat moss is often formed in whole or part from sphagnum in decomposed form. Also available, packaged, in whole pieces, dried or fresh; useful to line wire baskets and the like.

Sphagnum Peat. Containing a minimum of 66⅔% sphagnum fibers by weight (a peat which has been oven dried).

Spike. An elongated flower cluster having blossoms sessile (attached directly by the base) or on stalks that are unusually short.

Spore. A very simple reproductive cell able to produce a new plant (e.g., ferns and moss).

Spreader. A term used to describe a plant that grows wider than tall. Also referring to certain materials added to sprays to aid in distribution. A mechanism used for seeding and fertilizing.

Spreading. The procedure used to apply grass seed or fertilizer to soil or lawns by use of a spreading device.

Sprig. A small twig or shoot.

Sprout. The term used to denote the development of new growth from seed. Also the development of new shoots.

Staking. The practice of driving a pole or rod into the ground close to the stem of a young plant providing support during its vertical growth.

Standard

Standard. A shrub, herb or tree which has a single upright tree-like stem. Also refers to the upper,, usually upright petal of an irregular flower.

Starch. A white odorless, tasteless compound formed from sugars. In plants, starch is the main storage form of carbohydrates.

Starter Solution. A chemical fertilizer first dissolved in water, then applied in the planting hole or around the roots of seedlings that have been newly transplanted. Helpful in withstanding the shock of being moved, it also speeds up the seedlings' development.

Sterile. The condition of plants that are unable to reproduce, either because their seeds cannot germinate or because they do not bear any fruit. Sterile soil means that the soil is free of living organisms (barren soil).

Sterilize. This means ridding the soil of fungi, bacteria, worms and other living organisms in the soil which are harmful to plants.

Stolon. A horizontal branch from the base of a plant that produces new plants from buds at its tip. It creeps along the surface of the ground, rooting now and then and forming new plants (e.g., Bermudagrass).

Strain. A group of similar plants of the same variety with a common characteristic of improved growth or quality e.g. size, color, vigor or disease resistance.

Stress. The external factors that inhibit perfect plant growth, i.e. all factors pertaining to the wide ranging conditions of nature and man's understanding, knowledge and experience in contending with these conditions.

Subirrigation. The practice of watering from underneath. Such irrigation ranges from elaborate watering systems through conduit beneath the ground, to simply placing a newly potted plant in a tray of water to absorb moisture by capillary action. Also see Drip Irrigation.

Subsoil. The layers of soil lying beneath the 6-8 inches of topsoil often more compacted, less fertile, and containing less organic matter.

Succession. This means the normal sequence of crops, from cool-weather kinds (e.g., lettuce, peas) to warm-weather varieties (e.g., corn, beans) to cool fall varieties like cauliflower or cabbage. Succession can mean a wide variety of vegetables for one's dinner menu if the gardener plants small amounts of the same vegetable at frequent intervals.

Succulent. A plant having thickened, juicy stems or leaves (or both) which act as depositories of moisture against a time of drought. Its native habitat is the hot, dry desert regions. A succulent makes a fine house plant requiring little care.

Sucker

Sucker. A shoot which springs up from underground, grows from trunk or branch or the lower part of a plant — an unwanted shoot.

Sun Scald. When radiant heat from the sun strikes a newly exposed or frozen plant or the fruit of a plant, tissue is destroyed and the plant or fruit is said to be sun-scalded. A plant may appear to have sun scald if subjected to very high summer temperatures or extreme winter cold, resulting in damage to the bark. Also see Scald.

Systemic. A pesticide that is obsorbed into the system of a plant causing the plant juice to become toxic to its enemies.

Tamping. The practice of firming loosened soil into which seeds or new transplants have been placed.

Tap Root

Tap Root. A main root descending downward in the soil and giving off small lateral roots. Examples: carrots, dandelions.

Taxonomy. The science of classification, identification and description of plants. See Nomenclature.

Tender Plant. A plant which is injured or killed by even a light frost, or too much heat.

Tendril. A leafless threadlike organ on many vines which helps the vine to both climb and cling to its support.

Tendril

Terrarium. An indoor plant container made of transparent glass or plastic which can be covered to preserve needed moisture.

Thinning. The removal of some plants from a row so that the remeaning plants will have more room to grow and develop.

Top-dressing. The application of topsoil, fertilizer, compost or mulch material to the surface without mixing in.

Topiary (pruning). The technique for shaping trees and shrubs into formal or unnatural shapes (e.g., geometric designs, animals, etc.).

Toxic Material. Poisonous materials used to kill pests or those materials which may be poisonous to the growing plant.

Trace Elements. Minute quantities of mineral nutrients present in soil that are as vital to plant life as are the major nutrients. Examples of trace elements are copper, iron, manganese and zinc.

Training. The gardener's term for the many ways of pruning, pinching, staking and generally shaping growth into a desired form or shape.

Transpiration. The process by which moisture is emitted from plant leaves through transmission of water absorbed through its roots, dictated by humidity and temperature and available water.

Transplant. A plant produced from seed germinated in a favorable environment for later planting in an area where the plant is to grow to maturity. As seedlings begin to crowd, they should be transplanted to a second flat or container and allowed enough space to grow to three or four inches. They are then ready to be set out in the garden.

Trellis. An open structure of lattice used to support and train plants and vines as desired.

Tuberous Root. A true root that grows underground to serve as a food storage structure. It bears no buds or eyes.

Turf. A dense or matted growth of grasses with intermingled roots that form a mat.

Turgid. A term used to describe plant cells having adequate moisture to cause the cells to fully expand.

Variegated

Variegated. Refers to different colors (atypical) in leaf, flower or less frequently in fruit (e.g., alternating or scattered colored stripes, patches, etc.).

Variety. This means a subgroup of plants in a species (the lowest or final natural classification) with particular like characteristics. Each variety within a species keeps the basic character of the species, but has at least one, sometimes more, individual characteristics of its own. Manmade varieties are developed by cross-breeding the parents of different species. (See Cultivars).

Vermiculite. A mica product expanded by heat treatment to form an extremely lightweight material. It is used either for soil conditioning or as a rooting medium for plants. It is a product often used in a synthetic soil formula.

Verticillium Wilt. A fungus disease usually found in cooler climate areas which primarily attacks trees as well as a multitude of plants, resulting in slow wilting and eventual death.

Viable Seed. A seed containing a small living plant which will begin to grow once conditions necessary for germination (sprouting) are provided.

Weed. A plant growing out of place.

Wettable Powders. A mixture in which a toxicant is thoroughly blended with a filler with a wetting agent added to allow mixing with water. The toxicant is in a dust formulation and the water, rather than the filler, serves as the carrier. The particles of toxicant and filler are held in suspension in the water, but agitation is needed to prevent settling. Some kinds can be dusted on. See Dust.

Whorl. A circular arrangement of leaves, flowers or branches that grows from a node (joint) on a trunk or stem.

Windbreak. A dense planting, generally of evergreens or large shrubs, located so as to resist undesirable winds, providing protection for other plants, patio areas, etc.